THE WORLD OF MUSHROOMS

THE WORLD OF NATURE

THE WORLD OF MUSHROOMS

Adapted from the Italian of
UBERTO TOSCO

With a foreword by Ian Tribe

BOUNTY BOOKS
A Division of Crown Publishers, Inc., New York

Contents

List of tables

Foreword

The English language has a built-in confusion when it comes to dealing with mushrooms and toadstools, since both words are used indiscriminately and very few people know what the difference is. In many other languages there exists only one general word for these organisms: words such as champignon and fungo, for example. Are they distinct groups? Or are toadstools a type of mushroom, or vice versa? The general belief seems to be that mushrooms are edible, whereas toadstools are not. This is as much a nonsense as the notion that you can tell a poisonous species by its ability to turn silverware black. Generally speaking, most authors would accept that 'toadstool' refers to all the larger fungi, with 'mushroom' describing the small group of toadstools containing the edible mushroom and its close relatives.

The scientific names are, in theory, internationally accepted. In practice they are not, because the understanding of these fungi has improved greatly in recent years and not every authority yet agrees. The difference between old and recent books is in consequence often remarkable. Because of this problem you will find many alternative Latin names in this book. This tells not only about the history of the subject but also enables anyone to refer from one book to another without unnecessary confusion. The notorious case of the true mushrooms is worth recalling. Originally, mushrooms were placed in the group, or genus, called Agaricus; the name was then changed to Psalliota and has now reverted to Agaricus once more. This sort of confusion is of no help to any one trying to identify a particular toadstool. In this book, therefore, the alternative names have been given wherever it could be useful. At the same time, the English names have been quoted wherever they are widely used. Very few species have acceptable English names and one has to resign oneself to becoming familiar with the Latin.

Being able to identify a species correctly is obviously important; even more so if you are going to eat it. The rules for collecting and eating toadstools are set out in this book and it is important to read them carefully. Even if a species is described as edible, it is just possible that you may be allergic to it, or you may eat more than is good for you. So be warned: the first time you try a new species, only eat a small amount of it. Most importantly, it is never really safe to eat any toadstool without having the identification checked by an expert. Much of the task of identification is a question of accurate observation, and this also applies to spotting the less noticeable species. Once you have become used to looking out for toadstools and correctly identifying them, you will be surprised at how many more different types you will see.

Of course, eating toadstools is only one aspect of this fascinating subject. The variety of shape and colour is well worth studying and it naturally makes any walk or visit to the country much more enjoyable. Toadstools play a much larger part in the cycle of nature than most people realize. They are responsible for the breakdown of all manner of waste materials, returning substances to the soil for future use. They also live in partnership with plants, enabling both to exist where neither would be adequate on its own.

IAN TRIBE

v

Index of fungi

Page references to photographs are printed in *italics*; those followed by 't' are references to tabular material.

Index (continued)

Glossary

Adnate Type of gill attachment where gills and stalk are in contact throughout the depth of the stalk.

Annulus Type of ring found on the stalks of many toadstools.

Ascus Special reproductive cell producing its spores internally, typical of the *Ascomycetes*.

Basidium Club-shaped cell which produces spores externally and is typical of the *Basidiomycetes*.

Cortina Cobwebby veil stretching between the stalk and the cap edge, as in *Cortinarius* species.

Decurrent Type of gill attachment where gills run some distance down the stalk.

Eccentric Descriptive of a stalk which is joined to the cap on one side rather than in the centre.

Glaucous Dull greyish-green or blue.

Gleba Internal mass of spore-producing cells found in *Gasteromycetes* and truffles.

Hymenium Fertile layer containing reproductive cells (asci or basidia).

Papillate Having one or more small projections. In toadstools this may occur at the cap edge or on a central part of the cap.

Saprophyte An organism which feeds on dead material.

Symbiont An organism which lives in collaboration with another organism.

Sinuate Type of gill attachment where there is constriction in the lower edge of the gills near the point of attachment to the stem.

Stipe Synonymous with stalk and stem when describing toadstools.

Umbo (hence **umbonate**) Central swelling of the cap of a toadstool, rather like the boss of a shield.

Villous Covered with long, soft hairs.

What are fungi?

It is usually assumed that toadstools are plants, though this point is in fact debatable. Numerous and varied, they constitute the major group of Mycomycetes or fungi and it is worth mentioning that, when speaking of fungi, we are constantly using terms which begin with the syllable 'myco'. This is derived from the Greek 'mykes' which means 'fungus'. Thus 'mycology' is the science, or study, of fungi.

If fungi are plants, they are unusual in that, contrary to most others and certainly to all green plants, they are unable to draw all the nutrients which they need in order to live either from the soil or from any other inorganic material.

We know that plants thrust their roots into the soil in order to absorb the water around them. This water contains many elements, namely nitrogen, carbon, potassium, phosphorus, iron, zinc, magnesium and many others. These minerals, once absorbed, form the basic materials which eventually reach the leaves. Here they are converted into complex materials by means of the energy provided by sunlight and the carbon dioxide present in the air, which enters the leaves

A fine example of the Fly Agaric, Amanita muscaria. *This is a poisonous species but its beauty and structure of cap and stalk are represen-ative of many of the toadstools described in this book*

through minute pores called 'stomata'.

This results in food, rich in organic nutrients, which travels to all parts of the plant, giving them the means by which to live, grow and function. In fungi, however, the pattern is not quite the same. Green plants are autotrophic, or self-sufficient, while fungi are heterotrophic, or incapable of living on their own.

By 'toadstools' we usually mean those fungi which have a stalk and a cap, and are found in summer and autumn in woods, glades, fields and pastures, and sometimes in gardens, green-

(Below) this shelf or bracket fungus (Polyporus giganteus) lives on the base of tree trunks. Cap and stalk are almost indistinguishable

houses and compost heaps. Yet this is to generalize, since the particular fungi mentioned above belong only to the higher classes (macrofungi) and so form only part of the picture.

There are many types of fungi which do not have a cap and a stalk. Some have a kind of shelf

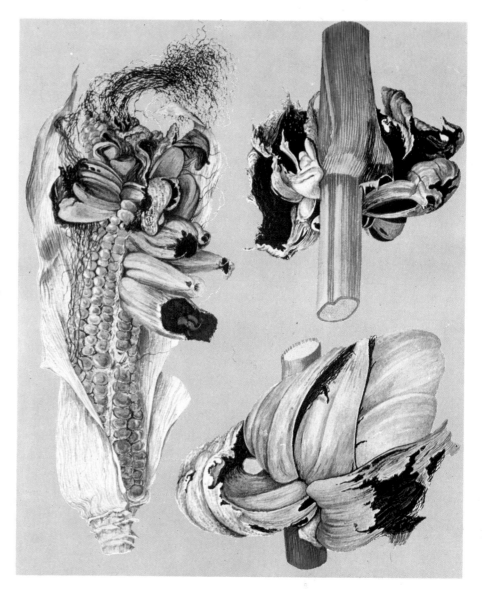

(Above) sweetcorn, or maize, is attacked by a number of rusts and smuts. These are microscopic fungi which feed on the fruits and eventually develop into swollen masses containing black spores

(Left) there are numerous fungi which grow on wood. Stereum hirsutum and various Corticium species are commonly found on dead wood

or bracket which is embedded into the bark of trees, sometimes singly, sometimes in groups. These are frequently large and coloured, generally solid and of a woody, corky texture. They may behave as parasites on dying trees, drawing food from the tree into themselves, or they may live off the dead tree as 'saprophytes'.

Some fungi have crusts and contain many tiny pores. These stain bark and wood, sometimes after it has been used as timber, flooring, etc. A third type consists of the thousands of minute fungi which frequently damage, disfigure or kill plants outright, even shrubs and trees. These fungi, while microscopic if considered from a structural point of view, have an effect out of all proportion to their size. This can be seen in many different ways, for example: the black tumours of maize; the spots and striped leaves of cereal rusts; the grey or green moulds which attack citrus fruits, pears and apples; the white, cottony threads which disfigure vegetables and fruit. Among these microscopic organisms are fungi which cause the peach leaf-curl and the peronospora of vines and potatoes.

3

There are also fungi which cause things to ferment, for example, the yeasts which use a special chemical process (alcoholic fermentation) to convert the 'must' in wine and also to make beer, dairy products, etc. Furthermore, yeasts are very simple fungi which, in many ways, are very close to the bacteria. In fact they can produce lesions on plants, animals and even man which are sometimes mistakenly thought to have been caused by microbes in the strict sense. Examples include the fungi which attack the mucous membranes of babies, those which give rise to aspergillosis (a disease of the lungs) and the agents of many skin diseases such as ringworm.

At this point it is interesting to note that many of the microscopic fungi can be allied with bacteria, *Actinomycetes* and *Streptomycetes* in a group called the *Schizomycetes*. The distinction between bacteria and fungi at this level is very difficult and many experts do not agree. The

bacterium which causes tuberculosis *(Mycobacterium tuberculosis)* is one such example; its scientific name, made up from 'myco', meaning fungus, and 'bacterium', indicates the confusion.

Fungi also have affinities with algae and with protozoa. The *Archimycetes*, for example, do not have the web of white threads, called the mycelium, typical of fungi, but are unicellular and have various stages in their life history similar to those of simple algae. Among other things, *Archimycetes* cause Black Rot of cabbages and Black Scab of potatoes. The so-called *Phycomycetes*, a very mixed group of microscopic fungi which includes bread moulds, fish gill rots and mildews, owe their name to the original belief that they have affinities with the algae (phycon = algae and mykes = fungus).

The fungi which have an affinity with the protozoa are the *Myxomycetes*, the amoeboid fungi or slime-moulds. The odd thing about them is

(Opposite page) fine example of Boletus calopus, *which is inedible and is typical of the toadstools which have pores instead of gills*

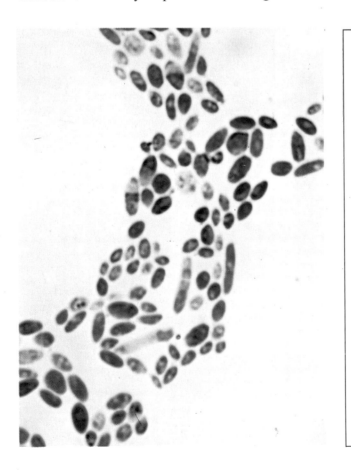

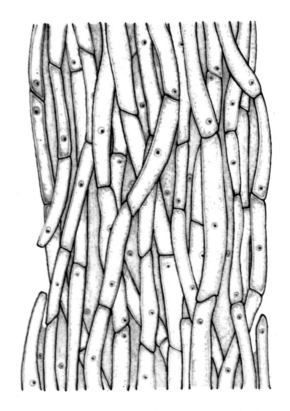

(Far left) a yeast, Saccharomyces cerevisiae, *seen under the microscope. This is one of the numerous microscopic fungi responsible for fermentation; this particular species produces beer. The cells have been stained with cotton blue to make them visible. Note that the cells are more or less separate. (Magnified approx. × 1000)*

(Left) portion of the stalk of a bolete showing the strands of long cells which make up a toadstool. Each strand is called a hypha (pl. hyphae) and together these make the mycelium and other tissues

4

that their naked cells slide over lawns, shrubs and fences in a slimy trail before they settle down to produce fruiting bodies. In this way the cells behave like *Amoeba*, the single-celled protozoan generally regarded as an animal. All dubious cases which are neither strictly fungi nor protozoa are put in a group called the *Mycetozoa*.

This book, however, is solely concerned with a small percentage of the many thousands of types of fungi. These, say, ten per cent comprise principally the best-known fungi: mushrooms, toadstools and cup fungi. The difference between mushrooms and toadstools is negligible, since the words are virtually synonyms. To avoid any further confusion, 'toadstool' will be used as the general term for all mushrooms and toadstools, although 'mushroom' may be retained for the small group containing the cultivated mushroom and its wild relatives.

The whole of the toadstool or cup fungus is made of many minute, white threads called hyphae, although in different parts of the fungus they have a different appearance. For example, the strands of the stalk are organized in quite a different way to those of the cap. Their ultimate job is to produce spores which will be scattered and grow into new fungi. Although spores are simple, usually single-celled objects, they can have a wide variety of shapes and colours.

The hyphae, each one only a few thousandths of a millimetre thick, can be seen easily in the mycelium. This is the cobwebby, or felt-like, white mass quite commonly found in the surface layers of soil, under leaf mould and in the bark of tree stumps and tree trunks. The 'spawn' which is sown when mushrooms are cultivated is really a chunk of mycelium in compost.

This mycelium can spread out over enormous distances. At certain points along it the young fruiting bodies appear. These are the result of sexual fusion between two nearby hyphae from the same mycelium or from two seperate mycelia of the same species. At first the fruiting bodies are small and button-like, but they eventually grow rapidly to become the toadstool or cup fungus as we know it.

The fruiting bodies of most large fungi are made of two distinct parts: the stalk, or stipe, and the cap, or pileus, as in the edible mushroom. The boletes (ceps), agaricas, russulas and ink caps are common toadstools with clearly defined stalks and caps. The shelf or bracket fungi, however, have no separate stalk and cap; the mycelium, embedded within the bark or wood of the tree, grows out into the fruiting body without forming a stalk. Similarly, the club fungi (*Clavaria* species) have no stalk and cap, but instead have a club-shaped fruiting body, as their name suggests. Puff-balls, jelly fungi and cup fungi are further examples of fungi without a stalk and cap.

Fungi also vary in size and texture. In fact, leaving out the microscopic fungi, there are mushrooms complete with cap and stalk which only measure a few millimetres in height. These live on dead leaves, rotting wood or dungheaps. Some, however, are larger than one might expect. Some clumps of polypores found on tree stumps (*Polyporus = Polypilus giganteus* and *Polyporus frondosus*, for example) can exceed half a metre in height or diameter, as can one of the puff-balls, *Lycoperdon giganteum*.

The texture of the fruiting body ranges from the gelatinous *Tremella, Auricularia* and *Peziza,*

Two gelatinous fungi: (above) a cup fungus (Peziza aurantia) and (right) a jelly fungus, Tremella mesenterica

(Above left) shelf or bracket toadstool, Daedalea quercina, *growing out of a tree trunk. No stalk is present*

(Left) fruiting bodies of Clavaria *species look rather like coral*

(Above) Clitocybe odora *is a small toadstool, easily recognized by its aniseed smell and its greenish tints*

(Left) Jew's Ear, Auricularia (= Hirneola) auricula-judae, *growing on elder, its usual host*

all jelly or cup fungi, to the delicate and deli-quescent flesh of the ink caps and the woody, corky bracket or shelf fungi.

As far as colour is concerned, the range is enormous. Some mushrooms are white, for example the Horse Mushroom (Agaricus arvensis) which the French call the 'snowball' mushroom for obvious reasons. Others are yellow or orange like the Chanterelle (Cantharellus cibarius) and Caesar's Amanita (Amanita caesarea), or red, such as several species of Cortinarius and Hygrophorus and the Fly Agaric (Amanita muscaria). Some, for example, Cortinarius violaceus, are a vivid violet colour. Most fungi, however, have a dull grey ochre or brown colour. Examples of green fungi, as in the extremely poisonous Death Cap (Amanita phalloides), are rare, and so too are glaucous fungi like Clitocybe odora. It is important to note that this green colour is not due to chlorophyll, the pigment normally found in green plants.

(Right) *the colours of some toadstools are vivid. This one,* Cortinarius violaceus, *is one of the most striking examples. It is harmless, but seldom eaten*

The reproduction of toadstools

Mushrooms reproduce by spores. When they are in the right conditions, namely: damp soil, good fertile manure, or warm humus, they germinate well and rapidly grow hyphae to form a mycelium.

An interesting point, however, is that the spores actually give rise to mycelia which, after special sexual processes, give life to numerous fruiting bodies, just as a seed produces a plant which can make numerous new seeds. The mycelium, therefore, appears to be comparable to a true plant, a single plant without distinctive organs.

The spores are produced in the fruiting body, either inside or outside, in special microscopic organs called asci and basidia. These are found in a special layer called the hymenium, which is, in the majority of cases, more or less exposed. The hymenium lines the gills which can be seen underneath the caps of many fungi. In the boletes and polypores, the hymenium lines tubes which go to form the spongy underside of the caps.

In other cases the hymenium covers the outside of the fungal body, as in the club fungi, coral fungi and the chanterelles, where it lines the folds. In the cup fungi, the hymenium is the inner surface of the cup.

There are, however, cases where the spores are completely encased by a fruit-wall and the only way they can escape is when this fruit-wall decays.

One example of this is the truffles, which live entirely underground and have an irregular shape. The spores are spread by earthworms, insect larvae or water.

There is no definite limit to the number of spores which a fungus can produce, for as the mycelium grows it produces more fruiting bodies. Production of spores is determined by the available food and other conditions such as temperature and humidity.

A great many fungi depend on the presence of higher plants for their future growth. Both partners benefit from this sort of relationship. The so-called 'fairy rings' are examples of mycelial growth in a regular and rhythmic pattern, fascinating to see.

Fungi can also reproduce by fragmentation of the mycelium, and this fact holds hope for the future cultivation of useful wild mushrooms, since mushroom cultivation is achieved by the inoculation of blocks of mycelium into the growth medium. Great care is taken these days to ensure the purity of the mycelium used.

(Below) fungal spores seen under the microscope. The etched surface of the spores is interesting and provides features which can be used to identify various toadstools. These particular spores are of a smut of wheat, Tilletia tritici

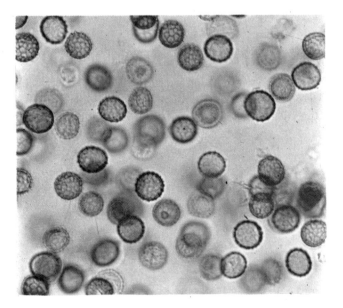

(Above left) group of a species of earth-star,
Geastrum rufescens (= G. fimbriatum) *which belongs
to the Gasteromycetes. The outer layer (exoperidium)
of the fruiting body splits open into 6–10 flaps,
revealing the spherical inner endoperidium. This opens
in a small pore, shown clearly in this photograph,
through which the spores escape*

(Above right) Boletus scaber, *one of the 'tube'
toadstools. The underside of the cap is covered in a
spongy mass of vertical tubes ending in minute pores.
The spores are formed in the tube linings and then
escape through the pores*

(Left) species of puff-ball, Lycoperdon perlatum. *As
in the earth-stars the spores are formed internally in a
brown or black powdery mass and escape through the
ruptured top of the fruiting body*

The classification of fungi

Mention has already been made of the micro-organisms which can be classed with either the bacteria *(Schizomycetes)* or fungi. Similarly, some fungi can be regarded as protozoa, others as a link with the algae *(Phycomycetes)*.

The true fungi, which are the concern of this book, produce their spores in a special fertile layer, the hymenium, either inside or on the outside of the fruiting body (known as the sporocarp). Each square millimetre of the hymenium can produce millions of spores; in some species several thousand are formed each minute. This production continues throughout the maturation of the fruiting body, releasing and dispersing the spores necessary to spread the species. The difference in the site of spore formation is important when the classification of fungi is considered.

Spores vary widely according to the species and differ in size, shape and colour. These differences can be seen between very closely related fungi as well as between fungi which are obviously distantly related. The way in which the spores are formed, and also where they are formed, is important in determining the group to which the fungi belong. There are two main classes of true fungi, the *Ascomycetes* and the *Basidiomycetes*.

In the *Ascomycetes* the spores are formed, in groups of four or eight, inside special cells called asci (singular – ascus). The asci can be cylindrical, conical, club-shaped or rounded, and, when mature, release their spores either through a hole in the tip or by splitting.

The *Basidiomycetes*, however, form their spores externally on the reproductive cells, or basidia (singular – basidium), which have much the same shapes as asci. The tips of the basidia bear two or four pointed horns, or sterigmata, to which the spores are joined.

Spores produced by asci are called ascospores; those from basidia are called basidiospores.

As mentioned above, both asci and basidia are part of the fertile layer called the hymenium. Both types of cell are interspersed, within the hymenium, with small cells called paraphyses, which some botanists regard as immature basidia. The *Basidiomycetes* also have much larger cells called cystidia within the hymenium; these are sterile and have no known function.

(Right) Polyporus (= Polyporellus) squamosus *on a tree trunk. The spores are released from pores on the lower surface of the cap. This is a very large species, easily identified by the feathery scales on top of the cap*

Illustrations of the fertile cells belonging to the two main toadstool groups. On the left, below, is an ascus, containing eight spores, (Ascomycetes)*; on the right are basidia, showing the developing and mature spores, produced externally,* (Basidiomycetes)

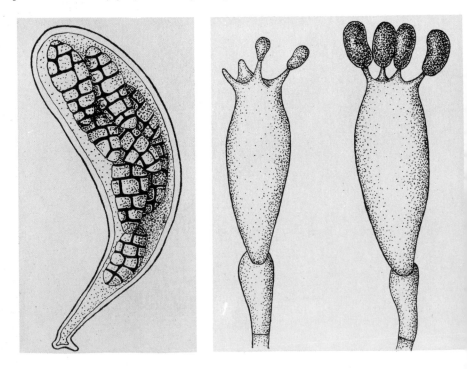

13

How and where toadstools live

It has already been said that fungi are heterotrophic organisms: that is, they are incapable of existing without complex organic substances, whether from an alive or dead source. Those which live on dead materials are said to be saprophytic, or saprobes; those fungi which feed entirely on living organisms are parasites, while some live as symbionts in mutual collaboration with other living organisms, mainly trees.

Saprophytic fungi are very common on all manner of dead remains: leaves, bark, wood and animals. Like the bacteria and protozoa, these fungi play an essential role in the cycle of nature by putting back into circulation all the materials required by autotrophic organisms such as green plants.

The parasitic fungi are those which live off other living things and often cause their death. Such fungi cause diseases of leaves, roots, stems, fruits, etc., and are often very specific as to which plant they will attack.

Symbiotic fungi are among the most interest-

Two toadstools which form mycorrhizas. (Below left) Amanita phalloides (Death Cap), the most deadly of all toadstools. (Below) Amanita rubens (= A. rubescens) which is edible only after cooking. Both species are found in a wide variety of woods

(Below) Boletus aereus. (Below right) Amanita gemmata (=A. junquillea). *The former is one of the most tasty toadstools, while the latter, though edible, is too easily confused with the poisonous Amanita citrina (=A. mappa) and care is needed*

ing because of the different ways in which they live with other organisms. Lichens, which are a mixture of fungi and algae, are a common example of this. Similarly, many fungi live with insects, particularly ants and termites, sheltering within their gut and digesting food which would otherwise be wasted.

Of all the symbiotic fungi, the most interesting are those which form the mycorrhizas associated with green plants: many trees, herbaceous plants, mosses and liverworts have them. The mycorrhiza is a layer of fungal threads, or hyphae, in very close contact with the underground parts of the plant, either growing within the plant or forming a sheath on the outside. In return for food, such as sugar, made by the green plant, the fungus supplies water and nitrogenous substances, together with salts of potassium and phosphorus which the plant needs and cannot always obtain in a soluble and directly usable form.

The existence of these mycorrhizas may limit

somewhat the species to be found in various conditions; those species which depend on trees and shrubs will only be found where their partners are also to be found. The range of toadstools in woods is therefore diverse, some being found in only one or two types of wood and others being of general occurrence. The situation is rather like the relationship between a parasite and its host: some parasites can only live with one particular host, whereas others will accept a wide range.

In spite of all this confusion, however, there are some very general rules which can be used as a guide to which toadstool to expect in a given habitat or situation. The number of toadstools present in woods is inevitably high, but their presence is affected by many considerations.

(Above) several specimens of Russula cyanoxantha, *an edible species often found in chestnut copses*

(Right) Russula lepida, *also found growing with chestnut trees*

Apart from all the species of tree and shrub which constitute a particular wood, other factors include the type of soil (principally because it determines the trees and other plants found there), and the amount of rainfall and waterlogging (very few toadstools will tolerate waterlogging; even after a very wet summer, few toadstools will appear). For this reason, the toadstool population of a particular type of wood may fluctuate from one district to another, and it will also be affected from year to year according to the weather. Toadstools do not necessarily fruit each year and this is why a crop, say, of Chanterelle may be plentiful in a wood one year and be completely absent the next.

Among the species which can generally be

(Above) examples of Lactarius deliciosus, *an extremely tasty species with an orange milk, frequently found in coniferous forests*

(Right) Amanita citrina (= A. mappa) *often occurring in chestnut and beech woods*

found in most kinds of woods are *Amanita rubescens* and *A. citrina, A. vaginata* (= *Amanitopsis vaginata*) and *A. fulva*; various mushrooms (*Agaricus* species); boletes such as *Boletus calopus* and *B. erythropus; Lactarius subdulcis; Laccaria laccata* and *L. amethystina; Clitocybe nebularis* and other clitocybes; *Marasmius confluens; Inocybe geophylla;* and various *Russula* species, including *R. nigricans, R. fragilis* and *R. ochroleuca.*

The coniferous woods, however, tend to have a specialized range of species which can tolerate the more acid conditions. In these woods, competition from other types of plant is very much reduced and the usually drier conditions are a distinct advantage. The species typical of such a habitat include boletes such as *Boletus bovinus, B. badius, B. viscidus* and *B. luteus; Lactarius deliciosus* and *L. rufus; Russula* species including *R. xerampelina;* as well as various *Cortinarius, Hydnum* and *Tricholoma* species.

Generally speaking, the toadstools found in broad-leaved woods are less specific as regards their tree partner. One reason for this is the fact that such woods tend to be rather mixed in their tree species. In this case, the lists of fungi for different types of woods or trees may overlap considerably. The broad-leaved woods are generally more fertile but vary enormously as to the soils on which they are found and therefore in the amount and type of ground vegetation which they support. The oak, for example, has a prolific ground layer of herbs and mosses which are often completely absent under beech trees. Among the most important species of toadstool found in broad-leaved woods we may mention *Amanita phalloides,* the Death Cap; *Boletus edulis, B. chrysenteron* and *B. subtomentosus;* the Chanterelle, *Cantharellus cibarius; Polyporus giganteus;* various *Russula* species, including *R. lutea, R. cyanoxantha* and *R. rosea;* together with *Hygrophorus, Marasmius* and *Psathyrella* species.

Specific associations between one type of tree and a toadstool can be found. For example, birch trees are usually associated with *Piptoporus*

betulinus, *Amanita muscaria* (Fly Agaric), *Boletus scaber* and *B. versipellis* and with *Russula versicolor.* The Jew's Ear, *Auricularia auricula-judae,* is always found on elder, so that anyone wishing to find this species knows immediately where to look.

Beech woods are not noted for many specific toadstools, but they contain a wide range of species, including many interesting and edible ones. The trees cast a shade which few flowering plants can tolerate, but which does not affect the toadstools. *Amanita phalloides, A. citrina, A. junquillea, A. excelsa, Russula lepida, R. cyanoxantha* and many other russulas may commonly be found among beeches. Species of *Cortinarius* and *Marasmius* are similarly common. Among the lactarii one may find *Lactarius blennius, L. zonarius* and *L. scrobiculatus,* while the clavarias and coprini are usually represented by *Clavaria pistillaris* and *Coprinus plicatilis,* respectively. The boletes are also well represented, particularly in the form of the Devil's Boletus, *Boletus satanas,* which is only found on chalky soils. Other boletes include *B. chrysenteron* and *B. aereus.*

This brief summary does not convey the enormous variety of toadstools found in woods. Apart from the fact that woods harbour the symbiotic and parasitic species, they are also

(Above) Yellow Bolete (Boletus luteus) *an edible toadstool frequently found in abundance in pine forests in company with* Boletus granulatus

(Above right) Blackening Russula, (Russula nigricans

(Right) Boletus elegans, *found in larch woods*

ideal habitats for other toadstools because of the increased warmth and shelter which they provide, and also for the amount of dead wood, animal droppings and leaves which all woods contain.

Among the saprophytic species there is a range of food requirements. Some toadstools, such as the Honey Fungus *(Armillaria mellea)*, will grow on any rotting stump, whether it be poplar, oak or beech, for example. Other species have more definite requirements: *Stereum hirsutum* will be found on hardwoods such as oak, but is never found on the softwoods such as pine or spruce.

The toadstools of grassy places, such as lawns, fields and clearings in woods, are also

special types not found elsewhere. The true mushrooms, *Agaricus campestris* and *A. arvensis*, are typically found in grassland such as grazed fields, but may also be found in a variety of other places. Similarly, the Parasol Mushroom, *Lepiota procera,* and the Fairy Ring Champignon, *Marasmius oreades*, are field species which may appear on lawns. The latter species is the one which typically produces the 'fairy rings' as dark green and brownish zones of grass. Originally, these rings were thought to be either supernatural phenomena or the effects of lightning, but they actually result from the growth of the toadstool mycelium outwards from the starting point in the centre. The circles enlarge over the years to be many metres in diameter.

There are numerous other species characteristic of grassy places; puff-balls, the blewits and the St. George's Mushroom, *Tricholoma gambosum.*

Heaths and other sandy places produce their own species, including those that are found mainly on burnt ground. On pure sand, however, such as sand dunes, very few toadstools are found; there is very little for them to feed on, since the only organic matter present is derived from dead animals or their droppings, or from decayed grasses.

The subterranean toadstools are a relatively small group, belonging to both the *Ascomycetes* and the *Basidiomycetes.* The best-known examples are the truffles. These are found associated with particular trees, but the traditional way to discover them is by the use of specially trained dogs, or even pigs.

The high organic content of animal droppings is obviously a most useful source of food for toadstools. The number of species found on dung (so-called coprophilous species) is surprisingly small but includes *Coprinus, Stropharia* and *Paneolus* species. Just as bare ground is colonized by a succession of herbs, so dung is colonized by a succession of toadstools, each species replacing the previous one in a definite order. The toadstools found on dung tend to be short-lived.

(Above) large group of Coprinus micaceus, *a species of ink cap. This is common in woods on rich soil*

(Right) Common Ink Cap (Coprinus atramentarius) *identified by its black and liquefying gills*

(Left) Beefsteak Fungus (Fistulina hepatica) *which grows, with or without a short stalk, on tree trunks. This toadstool is edible when young*

In conclusion one may say that toadstools live on a wide variety of sources, but all of them are organic. The food may be provided by a living organism, either willingly in exchange for other materials (symbiosis) or unwillingly, when parasitized.

Both types of feeding are commonly found in woods, but outside the woods symbiotic and parasitic types are uncommon, being replaced by saprophytic species.

Edible, suspect and poisonous toadstools

It is essential that anyone who collects toadstools, whether it be for scientific, commercial or gastronomic reasons, be able to identify the species correctly; quite apart from the scientific aspect, this is necessary because many species are highly poisonous.

It is not perhaps surprising that poisonous toadstools exist: after all, there are many poisonous flowering plants – Monkshood, Deadly Nightshade, Thorn-apple (Jimsonweed), Hemlock and so on – not to mention the poisonous animals such as vipers and some species of fish, spiders and insects.

In the case of poisonous plants and toadstools, the poison(s) gain entry to the body when eaten; with poisonous animals, however, the poison(s) are injected directly into the victim's blood stream by the animal. If an extract of a poisonous toadstool or other fungus is injected into the blood, the action is, of course, all the more rapid, quickly affecting the liver and the nerve centres of the body.

The poisonous content of a toadstool is not affected, like that of green plants, by the soil, the climate and other environmental factors. At first sight, the Fly Agaric appears to be an exception to this. It is collected and sold as a food in various parts of central Russia, whereas in most countries it is rightly regarded as extremely unpleasant to eat, if not fatal.

Just as there are races of the same species of plant found in different places, based, for example, on colour or size, so it is credible that races of differing poisonous qualities exist. This is known to be the case with flowering plants; the white clover has a race which is poisonous to slugs and another which is not.

In the case of the Fly Agaric, however, this does not appear to be the reason, since the Russians boil it before eating, and the skin of the cap is also removed, taking with it the bulk of the poison. Fortunately, the poison is water-soluble, so that by the time the toadstool is eaten it is quite harmless. Considering the enormous number of edible species, however, the risk involved in eating the Fly Agaric is probably not worthwhile.

It is comforting to know that edible species cannot become poisonous as a result of environment or contact with snails, slugs or poisonous animals such as adders. They can, however, in some cases become toxic as a result of ageing or damage by frost.

The net result is that a poisonous toadstool is virtually always so; only decay, age, and drying or cooking can affect it.

Through the ages, people have devised all manner of means to determine which species of toadstools are poisonous; crumbs of bread, parsley leaves, silver coins or silverware, have been, and possibly still are, used. The idea behind this is that the object will change colour if the toadstool is poisonous. These tests are absolutely useless. There are a thousand reasons why parsley leaves should turn yellow, or silver objects turn black, and it may or may not indicate that a particular toadstool is poisonous. Giving the toadstools to other animals is not a reliable test either, since each animal species is susceptible to varying degrees.

One cannot stress too strongly the importance of collecting, for edible purposes, only those toadstools which are known for certain to be innocuous. The basis for collecting must be a working botanical knowledge of any species which one wishes to eat.

In fact, there is a complete spectrum of toadstools from the most poisonous to those which are completely harmless. Among the most poisonous are the Death Cap, the Destroying Angel and the Fool's Mushroom. The Cep is one of the most widely eaten toadstools and very rarely has caused any form of illness. Where trouble has occurred, it has always taken the

Fly Agaric (Amanita muscaria) *a poisonous species, but not as deadly as its relatives,* Amanita phalloides, A. verna, A. virosa *and* A. pantherina. *Typical white spots on the cap are remains of the universal veil*

form of an allergy or rather upsetting gastric trouble.

Unfortunately, there is a very large number of poisonous species whose qualities have been most often discovered by their effect on susceptible individuals or on people suffering from heart conditions and other illnesses which might lower resistance to the poison.

The greatest number of toadstools belong to the class of 'suspect' species. This is not an easy term to define, nor is it a safe guide to edibility. The reason is that the effects often vary from one person to another.

The numbers of suspect fungi are swollen by the many species about whose edible qualities little or nothing is known. Even if it has only been recorded once that a certain mushroom has caused temporary minor illness, then that mushroom must, obviously, be suspect and hence should be avoided.

In the description of every species, therefore, mention is made of any precautions to be employed in dealing with the mushroom, whether to boil (thus removing water-soluble poisons and destroying heat-sensitive ones) or to remove the cap skin or stalk, and so on.

One unusual reaction, which is not properly understood, is the effect of frost. For example, the Honey Fungus, *Armillaria* (*= Armillariella*) *mellea*, which is one of the commonest of edible autumn fungi becomes, according to some French authors, poisonous or noxious if cooked after being frozen.

It is not clear, however, whether the frost directly causes the tissues to alter chemically to a poisonous condition, or whether it is part of the normal decomposition which immediately follows thawing in this species. The edibility of most species, however, remains unaltered by the action of low temperatures.

Lastly, one must add that some toadstools lose at least part of their poisonous qualities on drying. But even on this point research is somewhat fragmentary and could not be applied generally to the use of dried mushrooms either in the food industry or in the home.

(Above) Boletus luridus *is a 'suspect' species; it is eaten in some countries after cooking, but has occasionally caused minor poisonings*

Rules for collecting toadstools

1 Do not collect toadstools indiscriminately; pick only what is needed, either for eating or for further identification.

2 Identify carefully, then check, preferably with an expert. If you are unsure of your identification, leave the toadstool well alone.

3 Never eat more than a small amount of a toadstool the first time; you may be allergic to it.

4 Avoid any young toadstools since you may confuse them with other species.

5 Avoid old specimens which may be tough and may have started to decompose.

6 It is generally advisable to avoid toadstools which might have been attacked by frost.

Toadstools which change their colour

Many of the suspect toadstools change the colour of their flesh if broken. The boletes have many examples: *Boletus luridus* and the related *B. miniatoporus* and *B. queletii*; *B. purpureus* (*= B. rhodoxanthus*); the Devil's Boletus *(B. satanas)*; *B. cyanescens*; the Bay Boletus *(B. badius)*; the Brown Birch Boletus *(B. scaber)*; and *B. rufus*.

The changing colour of the flesh is not absolutely correlated with poisonous qualities; *Boletus cyanescens*, in fact, whose flesh becomes an intense bluish-indigo, is quite edible; while the Devil's Boletus, whose pale flesh changes to green-blue on contact with air, is poisonous.

The situation is further complicated by examples such as *B. purpureus*, whose flesh turns from sulphur-yellow or gold to blue immediately on breaking. This edible mushroom must be collected immediately before cooking, as it otherwise becomes slowly toxic.

Lastly we must mention that the flesh of the ceps which normally turns bluish on cutting, becomes 'liquid' and finally blackish on washing and cooking when the specimens are too old. This different colour reaction need not cause alarm; it can be useful as a way of assessing the condition of the specimens concerned.

The colour change seen in boletes does not always last long; it may quickly revert to the original colour. This makes it extremely difficult or even impossible to distinguish, for example, between various boletes when they are dried and mixed up.

The change in colour is related to chemical changes in the tissues, brought about by substances known as enzymes which act on complex chemicals in the toadstools on contact with air. In the case of many boletes, these enzymes require

A notable example of Amanita aureola, *which may be considered as a sub-species of* A. muscaria

copper to be present – hence they are called cupro-enzymes. The blue colour of many boletes, such as *B. luridus*, is due to a substance called boletol being attacked by the cupro-enzyme. The same thing happens if apple juice is applied to a cut surface on the bolete – it immediately turns blue; the apple juice contains the same type of enzyme, generally called an oxidase. In *Russula nigricans* the flesh turns pink and eventually black due to a chemical called tyrosine being attacked by another cupro-enzyme, tyrosinase.

(Above) three specimens of Boletus (=Xerocomus) subtomentosus, *which is edible and has yellow flesh that turns green-blue on cutting*

(Below left) the Peppery Milk Cap, Lactarius piperatus, *has white flesh and milk and both remain white even on contact with air*

(Below) Boletus cyanescens, *however, turns rapidly blue on cutting*

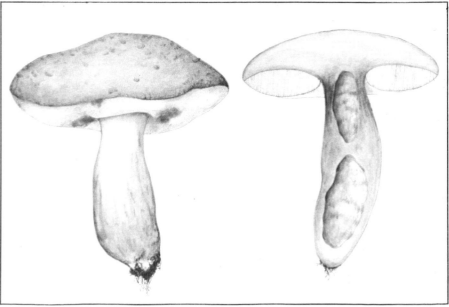

Toadstools with gills

It has already been said that fungi are classified according to the structure of their fruiting body, particularly in relation to the presence of asci, which contain the spores, or basidia, which produce spores at the tip.

Toadstools with gills are the most commonly seen larger fungi. They are members of the *Basidiomycetes* which have basidia, and generally have a stalk more or less in the centre of the cap. On the underside of the cap are the gills, which radiate out from the centre. The gills are lined with the hymenium, containing basidia with spores.

The *Basidiomycetes* with gills are put in their own major group, or Order, *(Agaricales)*, which is split into a number of families. The fungi are distributed among these families according to the colour of their spores. This colour does not always correspond to that of the gills, and there are brightly coloured gills bearing spores which are translucent or colourless and therefore appear white *en masse*. Spore colour can be most easily

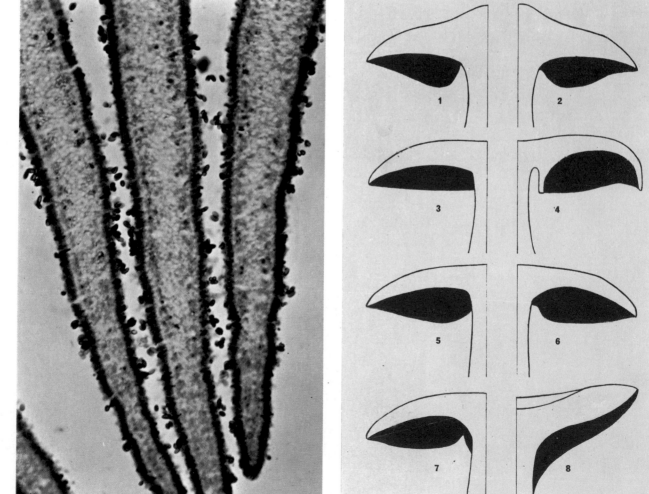

(Right) gills of a Coprinus *species seen in section under a microscope. The outer, darkly stained layer on each gill is the hymenium, containing numerous basidia and spores. (Magnification: × 150)*

(Far right) diagrams of types of gill: 1, distant; 2, sinuate; 3, adnate; 4, inserted on a collar; 5, annexed; 6, emarginate or umcimate; 7, decurrent; 8, strongly decurrent

found by removing the stalk and leaving the cap, gills down, on white paper overnight. A spore print will be formed, usually indicating the proper colour of the spores.

On the basis of the spore colour the following groups of families can be recognized: those with white spores (though some are cream or pinkish); deep rose-pink spores; ochre or brown spores; violet-purple spores; and lastly those with black or dark brown spores.

Another very important characteristic feature in classifying and recognizing the agarics is the relation between the gills and the stalk. In some species the gills are completely free of the stalk, while in others the gills may run for some distance down it (decurrent). In between, there are varying degrees of attachment to the stalk: annexed, where the gills just touch the stalk; adnate, where contact is made between gills and stalk through-out their depth; and sinuate where there is a constriction in the lower edge of the gills near the point of attachment to the stem. Decurrent gills are particularly noticeable and easy to recognize, being typical of the lactarii (milky caps).

The amanitas can be taken as suitable examples of agaric structure. The fruiting bodies are first recognizable as an 'egg' underground, covered in a white membrane known as the universal veil.

If one of these 'eggs' is cut open vertically, the universal veil, enclosing the young toadstool, can be clearly seen. The gills are also covered by a membrane, the partial veil. Both veils rupture as the toadstool expands and they generally disappear; in the amanitas, however, both remain as traces, the former becoming the volva (the split, shell-like structure at the base of the stalk) and the latter the ring, or annulus, towards the top of the stalk.

The presence of both ring and volva is typical of the amanitas. In *Amanita muscaria*, the Fly Agaric, the universal veil is also left behind on top of the cap as white flecks – for which this beautiful toadstool is famous.

In the amanitas, both stalk and cap are well developed, the stalk being central, and the cap,

(Above) Amanita (= Amanitopsis) vaginata *has an olive-grey cap, easily recognized by the marginal grooves*

although convex at first, becomes rather flat-tened. This genus contains a mixture of deadly and edible toadstools – hence the need to identify them correctly. For example, *Amanita phalloides* (Death Cap) and *A. virosa* (Destroying Angel) are lethal even in the smallest amounts, while *A. caesarea* (Caesar's Amanita) is one of the edible species, much prized in some countries. The first and last mentioned toadstools are often confused, as are so many of this group. *A. caesarea*, however, is alone among the amanitas in having a golden or sulphur-yellow fruiting body; the rest, including the Death Cap, are white or have delicate pastel shades.

Both *A. virosa* and *A. verna*, very closely related species, can be distinguished from *A. phalloides* by their slightly smaller caps, which are entirely white, and by their slender stalks. *A. virosa* has a noticeable nipple in the centre of the cap. These species can be distinguished from the edible mushroom by the following two characteristics: they have persistently white gills and *both* volva and ring are present.

The greatest confusion arises in the young

toadstools, when the colours and general shape have not yet developed. One means of distinguishing these three amanitas from *A. caesarea* is in the shape of the 'egg', or, rather, in the way in which it lies in the ground; that of the Death Cap and closest relatives has the pointed part upwards, that of *A. caesarea* has the point turned down.

Another group of amanitas is characterized

(Left) examples of Amanita vaginata, *variety* fulva

(Below) Caesar's Amanita (Amanita caesarea) *the only amanita to have yellow gills, stalk and ring*

(Below) section of a young A. caesarea

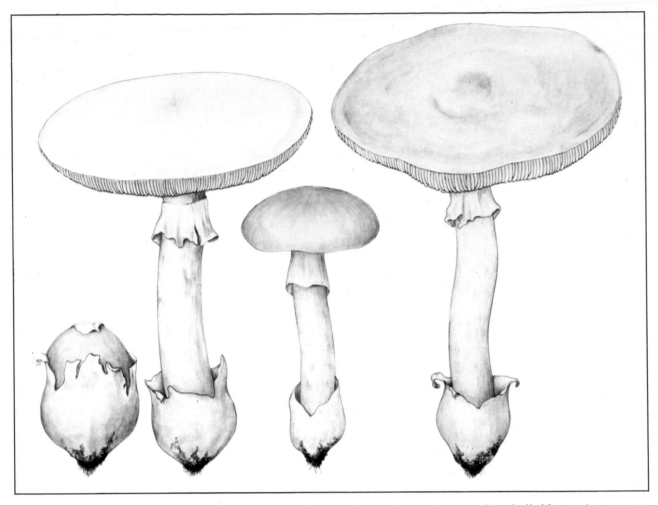

by the presence of white or greyish warts on the cap; these are the remains of the universal veil left when the veil ruptures as the toadstool grows, the lower part becoming the volva.

The easiest and most reliable way of recognizing toadstools with warts is simply the colour of the cap. In the Fly Agaric *(A. muscaria)*, the cap is a most attractive scarlet, becoming golden-red. Another feature is that the volva is not very distinctive and is rather rough. The common name of the toadstool, not surprisingly, is derived from its poisonous effect on flies, which are killed by the merest contact with substances present in the cap. It was at one time used for this purpose. This fungus is in any case generally poisonous, though not as poisonous as the *A. phalloides-verna-virosa* group. Very closely related to the Fly Agaric, and often treated as a variety of it, is *A. aureola,* which has a red cap but without warts.

Another species which does have warts on its brown or grey-brown cap is the Panther *(A. pantherina)*. The warts are pyramidal and not flattened like those of the Fly Agaric. The Panther is another very poisonous, even lethal, species which can be easily confused with two others: *A. excelsa,* whose cap is rather pale and covered in whitish warts; and secondly *A. rubescens (=A. rubens),* the Blusher, which

(Above) the deadly Amanita phalloides *varies a great deal in its colour. Here are shown variations from olive-green to cream, or pale olive-ochre*

(Below) Amanita virosa, *the Destroying Angel, seen entire and in section, is as deadly as* A. phalloides *but is much rarer. It has a distinctive shape to its cap*

becomes reddish as it ages, besides having flesh which, unlike the other two species, turns red on exposure to the air.

Amanita excelsa is edible; *A. rubescens* can be eaten with caution and only after cooking, which destroys the poison.

Also among the amanitas with warts we may mention the False Death Cap *(A. citrina = A. mappa)* and *A. gemmata (= A. junquillea)*; the former has a lemon-yellow cap, the latter has one which is golden-yellow turning to yellow-reddish and has a striated edge. Although it is edible, *A. citrina* was for a long time thought to be definitely poisonous albeit less so than *A. phalloides*. It has now gradually come to be accepted that it is harmless, though its similarity to the Death Cap is sometimes sufficient to cause confusion. The differences lie in the colour and the presence of warts, but both species are variable, and, in extreme cases, may overlap. For instance, the Death Cap itself varies a great deal in its colour, sometimes reaching a citrus-yellow, while *A. citrina* may be found with few or no warts, especially after heavy rain.

The Grisette, *Amanitopsis vaginata,* is completely harmless. It differs from the true amanitas in the lack of a ring on the stalk. This toadstool varies in cap colour from lead-grey to whitish or reddish. The cap is also striated at the edge, and the volva at the base of the stalk is very prominent.

The above poisonous amanitas are the most common, and the most interesting. There are many other species to be found in woods, but although they are less common they are none the less interesting, and well worth knowing.

One of these is *Amanita ovoidea* or *A. alba,* which is totally white and has much the same shape and size as Caesar's Amanita *(A. caesarea).* It differs in the size of the cap, which is sometimes 5–20 cm across, and is powdery or mealy without a striated edge. The greatest difference is in the stalk, which is white and also a little powdery. This fungus is edible, and found in both coniferous and deciduous woods in warm regions.

Amanita ovoidea could be confused with two other white amanitas, the deadly *A. verna* and *A.*

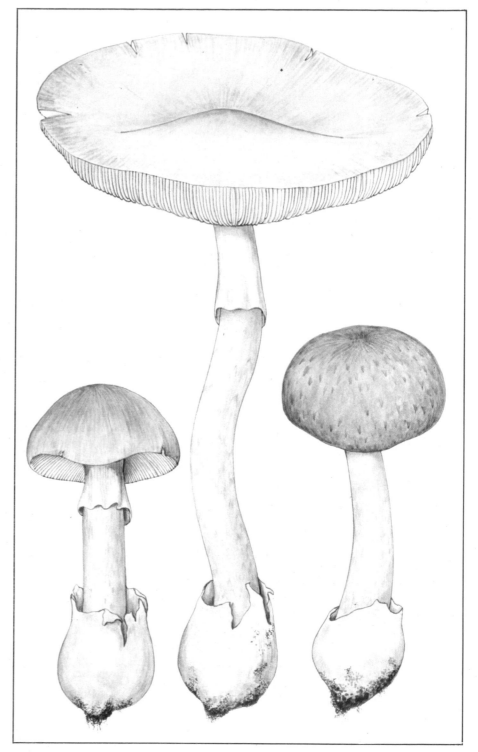

Colour variations of Amanita phalloides *(other than those opposite) include yellow, pale olive-green or olive-brown as shown above*

virosa, were it not for its relative size and the powderiness at the edge of the cap. Both features are sufficiently distinctive to prevent this confusion.

The last amanita we shall consider is *Amanita porphyria,* which is found, rather infrequently, in coniferous woods during summer and autumn; it is not a toxic species, but is often treated as such

(Left) various amanitas. (Top) two forms of the Fly Agaric, A. muscaria. *The usual one is on the far left; the one on the left is the golden form. (Bottom, far left) a young* A. aureola, *which differs from* A. muscaria *in not having warts on the cap; (left) the Fool's Mushroom,* A. verna, *a completely white and deadly species*

because it has an unpleasant taste reminiscent of *A. citrina* and *A. phalloides*. It is rather small, with a cap of 5–8 cm diameter which is at first convex or bell-shaped, becoming flattened later; its colour is brown, fringed with purple, and is darker in the centre. The gills are white and dense, while the stalk is slender, white, or fringed grey-violet and bulbous at the base; the ring is thin, white and grey-black and the volva is rounded and free.

Morphologically similar to the amanitas is the genus *Lepiota*, another group of white-spored agarics. The commonest is the Parasol Mushroom, *Lepiota procera*. It can be as much as 25–30 cm high; its stalk is whitish and has large brown-red scales which are numerous on the cap as well. The cap itself, which is umbrella-shaped, is 15–20 cm across. This is an edible fungus, but the tough stalks should be thrown away.

The ring is present to a greater or lesser degree in this genus and some species have white gills, as in *Lepiota* (=*Macrolepiota*) *procera*, *L. rhacodes*, *L. excoriata*, while others have red gills, such as *L. leucothites*. All of these species are edible.

We shall now deal in greater detail with a few of the lepiotas.

The Shaggy Parasol, *L. rhacodes*, has a cap which, as in the Parasol, is at first hemispherical and then becomes flattened. The cap is very scaly and is dark brown. The gills are free (not attached to the stalk), and are white flushed with red. The flesh is white, turning red on contact with air. The stalk is shorter than that of *L. procera,* and is hollow and not mottled like the Parasol. It is sometimes eaten but not often, and is found in summer and autumn, mainly in fertile, cultivated soil, and woods with a lot of rich leaf-mould.

An excellent fungus, which is especially abundant on moors, heaths, in pastures and in gardens, is *Lepiota excoriata.* It is of medium height, with a cap 5–15 cm across, which is rounded or ovoid at first, then becoming convex. It is an ochrish-grey colour, darker at the centre. The gills are

(*Above*) the flesh of Amanita rubescens, *the Blusher, turns red on exposure to air*

(*Left*) *a relative of* Amanita excelsa *and* A. rubescens *is* A. aspera, *shown here*

(*Right, top and bottom*) *examples of* Amanita spissa, *which has a greyish stalk in contrast to the white stalk of* A. pantherina

white and dense; the stalk is slightly enlarged at the base and is white or whitish, with a flared ring. The flesh is white, and has a pleasant taste, even though it is slightly perfumed.

Of the same size is another edible parasol, *Lepiota leucothites,* which has flesh-coloured gills. The cap is at first rounded, but quickly becomes flattened. The stalk is cylindrical, slender and thickened at the base, with a membranous, free ring high up. It is quite common in some places in the summer and autumn, being found most often in gardens, fields and pastures. Because of its white colour it could be confused with

These two illustrations demonstrate the differences between Amanita citrina *(above left) and* A. junquillea *(above right). The former is inedible and has a white cap; the latter is yellow and has a striated margin*

(Below) Amanita solitaria *is totally white and has a fringed cap*

the *Amanita verna-virosa* group, but it does not have a volva.

Among the less common lepiotas is *L. friesii* *(=L. acutesquamosa)*. This has a brown or ochrish cap covered in small scales, and is often regarded as poor in quality and not suitable for consumption. It can be found from summer to autumn especially in coniferous woods.

Rather smaller than the species already mentioned is *Lepiota clypeolaria,* which is also found in woods and is edible. Its cap is only 4–6 cm

(Above) young specimens of Amanita solitaria *showing the irregular fringe and large warts on the cap*

(Below) Lepiota procera *in two stages, first young and then the mature fungus, showing its free ring*

diameter, always umbrella-shaped, with an ochrish or yellowish colour and rather dark scales, especially towards the centre. The gills are white with a yellowish tinge, while the stalk is slender, slightly swollen at the base, white or greyish and somewhat scaly from the ring downwards.

There are also two very small lepiotas: *L. cristata,* and *L. helveola.* The first species has a cap 2–5 cm across, with a central nipple; it is white with small scales and an umbo (see glossary) of brownish-red. The gills are white and the dainty stalk is white or slightly ochrish. The ring is generally short-lived. This is a toadstool which grows in woods, gardens and orchards, and

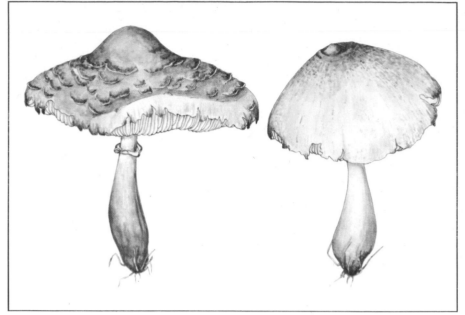

(Above) Lepiota badhami. (Above right) Lepiota excoriata (with warty cap and white gills) and L. leucothites, which has a white cap and pink gills

(Below) Lepiota mastoidea (= L. gracilenta) has a spotted, or brindled stalk

(Below right) Lepiota rhacodes, the Shaggy Parasol, has large warts on the cap

whose flesh has an unpleasant smell which makes it unsuitable for cooking.

Lepiota helveola is poisonous and is found in fields, gardens and forest glades, though it is quite rare. The cap is 3–6 cm across, convex becoming flat. Its colour varies from ochrish to red (it turns red on touching), and it becomes brown and cracked with age. The gills are white, the stalk is much lighter than the cap, and the ring is irregular and short-lived. The flesh is white

(Right) Lepiota friesii, *noted for the dark scales on its cap which are numerous in the centre*

(Below) Lepiota clypeolaria, *like all small lepiotas, is not really worth eating although it is an edible species*

but becomes red when it is exposed to the air.

Clearly related to both the white-spored amanitas and lepiotas are species of the genus *Volvaria* (or *Volvariella*), among which both *V. gloiocephala* and *V. bombycina* have a volva so large that it virtually encloses the stalk. However, they do not have a ring and their gills and spores are red. For this reason they are put among the red-spored agarics.

Also like the lepiotas, the true mushrooms (*Agaricus = Psalliota = Pratella*) lack a volva but have a ring. They are distinctive, however, because of the way in which the gills turn pinkish (or red-violet-grey) as they mature. The poisonous amanitas (e.g. *A. verna* and *A. virosa*) are

(Above) Agaricus silvicola *at various stages of development. Note the very pale colour of the cap*

(Above left) Agaricus silvaticus

(Left) Agaricus campestris, *the Field Mushroom*

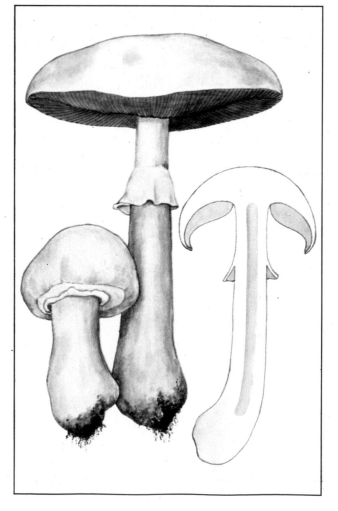

(Left) the Yellow-staining Mushroom, Agaricus xanthodermus, *entire and in section, showing the base of the stalk which turns yellow on cutting and the yellow patches which develop if this mushroom is rubbed. It can cause illness, lasting for several days*

either completely white, or, if they have colour it is restricted to a marbling of their stalks.

The mushrooms are generally edible, with the exception of the Yellow Stainer, *Agaricus xanthodermus,* which can cause illness lasting for several days. As its name perhaps suggests, it has the property of turning yellow on contact with air; this feature, however, is shown only by the base of the stalk, but it is a clear and immediate colour change. Also the skin of both cap and stalk will turn yellow if rubbed. The cap itself is white, with some brownish scales at the centre. The flesh has an unpleasant smell enhanced by cooking. Although not fatal, it is obviously best avoided.

Of the edible wild mushrooms, probably *A. campestris* (=*Psalliota campestris*), the Field Mushroom, is best known since it is certainly very tasty. The cap is white, while the gills are

On this page are shown various forms of the Honey Fungus, Armillaria mellea, which varies enormously in colour

pink, becoming brown. In the Horse Mushroom *(A. arvensis)*, however, the cap becomes yellowish as it ages and the gills are greyish. This second species is much larger than the others, being 15–20 cm across the cap; it also has a distinct smell of aniseed.

Two other species which can sometimes be confused with *A. xanthodermus* are *A. silvaticus* and *A. silvicola*. The first species has a whitish cap or yellowish-brown cap covered in red-brown scales, and the flesh turns red on exposure to air. The second species, popularly called the Wood Mushroom, has a flattened cap, 5–10 cm in diameter, which although white at first becomes yellowish as it ages. Like the Horse Mushroom, the flesh has a smell of aniseed, a feature which distinguishes it from the Yellow Stainer, besides the fact that it does not turn yellow at the base of the stalk.

Rhodophyllus sinuatus (= Entoloma lividum) is a poisonous toadstool with similar colouring to many of the mushrooms, having a dull, ochrish cap, white stalk and gills which turn from yellowish to pink as they age. It can be distinguished from the mushrooms quite simply by the fact that it has no ring. *Rhodophyllus prunuloides* is very similar.

Red gills and the absence of a ring are typical of *Pluteus cervinus*, which has a sooty-brown cap 3–8 cm across.

The Honey Fungus, *Armillaria (= Armillariella) mellea*, has a definite membranous ring which is spotted with yellow. It is an edible species, highly regarded by some people, and commonly found in clusters on stumps; it is also responsible for killing a lot of trees. The cap (3–10 cm) is yellow-brown with small scales, although the colour can vary considerably.

There are many other toadstools which grow

(Above right) Hypholoma sublateritium. *(Right)* Hypholoma fasciculare, *(and far right)* H. sublateritium. *These two poisonous toadstools can be confused with the edible Honey Fungus,* Armillaria mellea *shown on the opposite page*

in clusters, such as in the genus *Hypholoma*. The Sulphur Tuft, *Hypholoma fasciculare,* is not edible and has bright yellow caps with green gills. *Hypholoma sublateritium* is a much larger, suspect species with a reddish cap and brownish gills. Both species are relatively common.

Turning again to the genus *Armillaria,* two species must be mentioned which are related to the Honey Fungus *(A. mellea)* but are much larger. One is *Armillaria (= Catathelasma = Biannularia) imperialis,* which can be up to 45 cm across. It has an enormously thick stalk and a double, membranous ring. The cap is ochrish-grey in colour. Although edible, the smell of this species makes it rather unpleasant. The second species is *A. caligata (= Tricholoma caligatum).* It is not quite so large and also has a membranous ring half-way up the stalk. The lower part of the stalk is covered in fibrils which merge with the ring. In its smell and taste this is rather a variable species; some forms are palatable, others are disagreeable.

In the genus *Cortinarius* the loose fibrils on the stalk and edge of the cap become very pronounced and form what is called a 'cortina', a mesh-like, partial veil. There are numerous cortinarias, many of them having a swollen, almost bulbous, stalk base, and reddish gills and spores.

One of the most colourful cortinarias is *C. violaceus,* which is edible and has a distinctive violet colour, as one would expect. The gills are at first violet, becoming ochrish as the spores mature.

Somewhat less brightly coloured is *C. purpurascens,* which is relatively common from summer to autumn. The cap is 8–12 cm, convex and somewhat sticky, while it is brownish-violet in colour, often mottled. The gills are purple-violet, turning to brown-cinnamon as they age, but becoming a vivid violet if bruised. The stalk is rather short and violet-blue in colour, also

(Above left) Cortinarius purpurascens; *(left) young* Cortinarius praestans, *an edible fungus which can often reach a large size*

44

turning bright purple if bruised; it is noticeably swollen at the base.

Another brightly coloured *Cortinarius, C. (= Phlegmacium) caesiocyanus*, is found in woods, particularly on chalky soils. This edible toadstool has a cap which is at first convex, and then becomes expanded and humped. It turns from violet to violet-grey-blue, and even ochrish or

(Left) Cortinarius caerulescens *has a pale violet tint to the cap with cortina and spores of a cinnamon or hazel colour*

(Below) examples of Cortinarius alboviolaceus. *In the background is a* Lycoperdon perlatum

(*Above*) Cortinarius (= Myxacium) collinitus

(*Right*) Cortinarius fulmineus, *which has rusty scales on its cap*

Four Tricholoma *species: (top left)* T. flavovirens *and (top right)* T. rutilans; *(above)* T. vaccinum *and (above right)* T. gambosum

brown in the centre. The dense gills show much the same colour sequence. The base of the stalk is swollen, being violet-amethyst in colour at first, then ochrish. The flesh is violet on top and yellowish at the bottom.

Cortinarius (=Inoloma) alboviolaceus is a lighter-coloured species found especially in beech and oak woods on poor soils. The cap is a light, whitish-violet and the gills are grey-lilac to brown-red. The stalk is rather bulbous at the base, tapering towards the top. It has the same colour as the cap, with a smooth white veil which turns rough as the spores ripen and fall. The flesh is edible and tasty.

There are also many cortinarias which are yellow or ochrish. Of these, the Sticky Cortinaria, *C. (= Myxacium) collinitus*, is probably the most representative. It is edible, but not often eaten because of the sticky mucus covering the stalk. The cap, 4–10 cm across, is glutinous, and of a mealy-ochrish colour, which is lighter towards the edge. Its gills turn from white tinged with a pale grey-violet colour to ochrish-red as the spores ripen. The stalk is lighter at the top, becoming brown and scaly towards the bottom.

A palatable *Cortinarius* is *C. (= Phlegmacium) fulmineus,* quite edible but rarely used, of medium size and with a cap of 8–10 cm diameter. The sticky cap is convex and of a golden colour, while the gills are yellow at first. The stalk is large and thickened at the base, with a pale yellow cortina. The flesh is almost white, though the skin is yellow.

Somewhat similar is *C. melliolens*, common in woods in summer and autumn. It is smaller than the preceding species, having an ochrish cap and being darker at the centre. The gills are white to cream; the stalk is thick and bulbous, of a pale yellow colour with a whitish cortina. The flesh is white.

Cortinarias with bright colours include *Cortinarius cinnabarinus (= Dermocybe cinnabarina), C. sanguineus (= D. sanguinea)* and *C. phoenicius (= D. phoenicia)*. Generally of small size, the gills of these toadstools (and even the whole body of the fungus) are a brilliant red colour.

In spite of all the confusion that one might expect in trying to identify all these toadstools, they all have varying characters such as a volva, ring, cortina and warts, together with differing coloration, texture and taste which serve to make it relatively easy to distinguish them.

It is certainly true, furthermore, that with a little experience and reasonable powers of observation, it is possible to find further distinctive differences between them, either in the young toadstool or in the mature form.

This can be seen, for example, in the lactarii, the milky caps (*Lactarius* species), where the cap is initially rolled inwards, protecting the gills. When completely mature, the margin rolls out to some extent, while retaining some of its incurved character. The cap is at first spherical, becoming expanded and, in the majority of cases, funnel-shaped; this is also true of the russulas (*Russula* species).

But leaving lactarii and russulas for the moment, we should concentrate on other genera which form a classic group in their own right (since they lack a volva and ring), and so deal specifically with the genera *Tricholoma* and *Clitocybe*. These two names, however, are generally synonymous.

Among the edible tricholomas, the most important is *Tricholoma gambosum (= Calocybe gambosa)*, the much-prized St. George's Mushroom. It is found in spring growing alone and is of moderate size and sturdy. Its cap and gills are white, turning to cream, and very dense; the stalk is whitish. This toadstool, like many other tricholomas, is characterized by its strong, mealy smell (although not everyone can smell it), but in spite of this it is quite harmless and in some countries is commonly sold as food.

Tricholoma albobrunnea also has a strong, mealy smell, but has a reddish-brown cap. Its stalk is a mealy colour at the top and the same colour as the cap at the bottom. It is generally considered to be indigestible rather than poisonous.

Both *T. flavovirens* and *T. sulphureum* are bright yellow species, the latter more so, being a sulphur-yellow, as one would expect from its name. The former is edible and has a brown-tinged scaly centre; the latter is not, however, edible, and has a strong smell like gas.

Tricholoma (= Tricholomopsis) rutilans is more of a golden-yellow, the cap being covered in purplish scales. This toadstool can be as much as 12 cm in diameter and is found on tree-stumps. It is regarded as suspect and even poisonous.

Naturally, there is no shortage of poisonous tricholomas, among which are *T. pardinum (= T. tigrinum), T. virgatum* and *T. murinaceum (= T. sciodes)*. The first species is the most dangerous, but is only commonly found in the coniferous woods on mountains. The cap is convex, bell-shaped or even a little umbonate, with grey-brown scales. The gills are a greyish-white, while the stalk, which is quite tough, is white and villous (see glossary) at the top, though light ochre at the base. This dangerous species can be confused with an edible one, *T. terreum*, but the latter is smaller and has a rougher appearance.

Among the other common tricholomas is *T. columbetta*, a medium-sized toadstool found on acid soils which is completely white. This one is edible. The cap is fleshy and smooth, somewhat flattened, and spotted with blue in old specimens. The stalk is tapered at the base, and can be a glaucous green in colour.

Tricholoma acerbum may occasionally be confused with *T. gambosum*. Its quality as a food is, however, poor, and it should be cooked first. The

cap is distinctive, being 6–12 cm diameter and compact, of pale ochre colour, sticky and darker in the centre. The gills are cream-white, becoming reddish if bruised. The stalk is short and cylindrical, whitish with small yellow scales at the top.

Another edible tricholoma is *T. saponaceum,* found growing in clumps or circles in woods. It is a very variable species, but none the less recognizable by its soapy smell. Generally it has a convex cap which may be rather undulating, grey-green or olive-ochre (even yellowish or white), darker

(Above left) Tricholoma acerbum; *(above)* Tricholoma saponaceum

Two edible tricholomas: (below left) Tricholoma terreum *and (below)* T. columbetta

in the centre; the gills are whitish, tinged with
green, while the stalk is cylindrical, white and
with a smoky-green or red tint at the base. The
flesh not only smells of soap, but has a bitter
taste. Although not poisonous as such, this
toadstool is best ignored.

We have already mentioned various toadstools
which can be confused with *Rhodophyllus sinuatus*; in one form it is very much like various
tricholomas, and although the gills of these may
be lightly coloured the spores themselves are
always white and not red. Close examination,
including a spore print, may therefore be required
to make the differentiation.

Although *Rhodophyllus sinuatus* is poisonous,
other members of the genus, such as *Rhodophyllus clypeatus* (= *Entoloma clypeatum*), are
edible. This particular species grows, in groups,
symbiotically with cultivated plants, especially
apples and pears. The related *Rhodophyllus
nidorosus* (*Entoloma nidorosum*) is, however,
suspect; this can be recognized by its smell of
ammonia.

Another edible *Rhodophyllus* is *R. nudus*
(= *Tricholoma nudum* = *Lepista nuda*). It is very
good to eat, in spite of its bright violet colour, and
is found during both autumn and winter in grass,
especially in coniferous woods. The spores appear
red or lilac *en masse*, but seen under the microscope they are transparent. The cap may even
appear ochrish in mature specimens, while the
gills are violet-brown. These features enable the
toadstool to be distinguished easily from *Corti-*

narius violaceus, which is also edible and brightly
coloured but has violet gills which become rusty.

While on the subject of unexpected colours
found in toadstools, *Clitocybe odora* (= *C. viridis*)
might be mentioned. It has a glaucous (see
glossary) green cap and the gills are whitish. The
flesh emits an agreeable, fresh smell of aniseed.

The genus *Clitocybe* has so many species, in
fact, that any discussion of this group must be
restricted to the most important ones.

Clitocybe nebularis is a common autumn species
in woods, especially among conifers. Its cap is up
to 15 cm or even 20 cm across, at first convex,
becoming flattened and perhaps concave, it is of a
grey-brown colour. The stalk is thick, but tapers
slightly towards the top. The gills are serrated and
more or less decurrent.

A related species is *C. aggregata* (= *Tricholoma
aggregatum* = *Lyophyllum decastes*) which forms
clusters in woods during summer and autumn.
The cap ranges from grey-brown to a darker
brown. Like *C. nebularis,* it is a large species, up
to 12 cm. It is edible.

Another *Clitocybe* which grows in clusters is

(Above) Rhodophyllus nidorosus, *a 'suspect' species, which can be recognized by its nitrous smell*

(Above right) *an edible autumn species,* Clitocybe nebularis

(Below) Clitocybe aggregata (= Tricholoma aggregatum). *The colour of the cap varies from grey-brown to dark brown*

C. (= Armillaria) tabescens, superficially very similar to the Honey Fungus, *Armillaria mellea,* but differing from it in the complete absence of a ring; it is also less common. This species is, in fact, frequently grouped in the same genus as the Honey Fungus and called *Armillaria tabescens.*

Two small clitocybes deserve a mention. These are *C. rivulosa* and *C. dealbata.* Both are whitish and found in grassy places and both are very poisonous, like various other white clitocybes. They can be distinguished from each other by the flesh-pink tinge of the first species, which also has a zoned cap. Unfortunately, they can be confused with edible species such as *Marasmius oreades,* the Fairy Ring Toadstool, and *Clitopilus prunulus,* which has cream or reddish gills.

One of the largest species of *Clitocybe* is *C. geotropa,* quite frequently found in wood clearings and pastures during autumn, sometimes in rings. It can grow up to 20 cm in diameter, with the convex cap becoming flattened and slightly concave to leave a central, raised nipple (umbo). The cap colour is pale ochre, the same as the gills, though darker than the stalk. The stalk itself is longer than the cap width and shows a slight tapering towards the top. Its lower part is covered with cottony fibres. This edible species produces a pleasant smell, but the stalks are tough, and it is therefore better not to eat it.

Even larger than the previous species is the closely related *C. (= Leucopaxillus) gigantea,* which grows up to 30 cm in diameter and is cream coloured. The stalk of this toadstool is

(Right) Clitocybe geotropa *can measure 20 cm in diameter.* (Centre) *poisonous* C. olearia, *found on olive trees.* (Bottom right) Clitopilus prunulus, *which can be distinguished from two similar, but poisonous, species,* Clitocybe rivulosa *(drawing, below left) and* C. dealbata *(below right), by its pinkish gills*

proportionately much shorter than that of *C. geotropa.*

There are various other clitocybes with concave or funnel-shaped caps, such as *C. infundibuliformis (=C. gibba)*. This is an edible species common in coniferous woods from summer to late autumn, with a cap which changes from convex to funnel-shaped. It has an inrolled edge in young specimens which becomes wavy at maturity. The cap is 4–8 cm in diameter, and tan or yellowish in colour; the white gills are crowded and decurrent, while the stalk is slender, of the same colour as the cap, hairy at the base and fibrous in old specimens. The flesh is white and has a characteristic faint smell like prussic acid.

Related to this species is *Clitocybe (=Cantharellula) cyathiformis,* distinguished by the colour of the cap, which varies from bistre to grey-brown. This is another edible woodland species, with a deeply funnel-shaped cap; it is found from autumn to early winter. Similar shape and

(Above) Clitocybe infundibuliformis, *rather more yellow in this case than is normal*

(Below) Collybia velutipes

(Below right) Marasmius oreades, *the Fairy Ring Champignon, useful as a condiment*

colouring is found in *Clitocybe (= Lepista) flaccida,* though the colour in this case is more reddish-brown. The cap is 4–10 cm and leathery; the stalk is relatively short, woolly at the base, and has colouring similar to that of the cap, or slightly lighter. This edible toadstool grows in groups in coniferous woods.

The gills are always an orange or orange-red colour in *Clitocybe (= Hygrophoropsis = Cantharellus) aurantiacus;* the cap is of a similar colour. This edible species was thought for a long time to be poisonous; there has also been confusion, as one can see, concerning the correct group in which this toadstool should be placed. The gills are decurrent and the cap is funnel-shaped, as in clitocybes, but the gills are forked and the toadstool can be confused with the Chanterelle *(Cantharellus cibarius)* if one is not careful. Unlike the Chanterelle, however, this species does not have an apricot smell.

There are many other genera of white-spored agarics, too numerous to deal with. The most important remaining ones are: *Collybia, Marasmius, Melanoleuca, Laccaria, Hygrophorus* and *Pleurotus.*

The genus *Collybia* is characterized by a convex cap and incurved edge, the gills sometimes being widely spaced, but never decurrent. *C. fusipes* is a summer-fruiting species found on beech and oak stumps. The cap is convex, slightly wavy, and a very dark brown-red, which fades with age. The gills are widely spaced, sometimes fused and being lighter in colour than the cap; the stalks are fused and grooved, and are a very dark colour. In the young form, various authorities consider this an edible species, but it is best ignored in view of a few reports of gastric upsets.

Collybia maculata, however, is totally different in colour, being whitish at first but becoming spotted reddish brown, especially if touched. It is a bitter toadstool and hardly worth eating.

Flammulina velutipes (sometimes classed as *Collybia velutipes*) is easily recognized by its cylindrical stalk. It is a very pale ochrish-yellow at the top, but is dark brown-blackish lower down. The cap is 3–6 cm broad, slimy and yellow-ochre which is darker and more orange at the centre. The gills are a pale yellow. It is edible and forms tufts on elm, ash and willow stumps from autumn through the winter.

A small toadstool commonly found in grass as rings or clumps throughout much of the year is the Fairy Ring Champignon or Toadstool,

Two views of Laccaria laccata, *a small edible toadstool which varies in colour from ochre-red (left) to violet, as in the variety* amethistea *(below)*

Marasmius oreades. It has a slender but tough stalk and a tan or buff cap of 2–6 cm. The cap is convex at first, becoming flattened with a central nipple; the gills are widely spaced and free; they are white at first but later buff coloured. Unlike the genus *Collybia*, to which *Marasmius* is otherwise very similar, the fruiting bodies can be dried without losing their properties. In the dried form, *M. oreades* is useful as a condiment in stews and soups.

Another small, edible toadstool is *Laccaria laccata* which, in size and general appearance, is reminiscent of *Marasmius oreades*; the stalk is nearly the same colour, and a little crooked. The cap is convex while the gills are widely spaced and paler than the rest of the toadstool.

The genus *Hygrophorus* consists of fleshy, brightly coloured species; in many cases the gills are waxy and widely spaced, while the cap may be sticky. *Hygrophorus* (= *Limacium* = *Tricholoma*) *russula* illustrates the history of many hygrophoras, since it was for a long time placed with the tricholomas. The purple cap is fleshy and convex, later becoming flattened. The gills are slightly decurrent, white or tending to red, and spotted with purple. This colour characterizes the stalk, which has a fine down at the top. This edible toadstool is found in deciduous woods in North America.

Hygrophorus agathosmus, found in coniferous woods in autumn, is edible but of little value. The cap is convex and light grey in colour, reaching 3–8 cm in diameter, while the stalk is thick and white. The flesh has a smell like bitter almonds.

Hygrophorus species with brownish caps include *H. olivaceoalbus*, with white gills, and *H. hypothejus* with yellowish gills. Both are edible, but of poor quality (like most hygrophoras) and

Three common species of Hygrophorus *(top to bottom)* H. russula, H. marzuolus, H. agathosmus

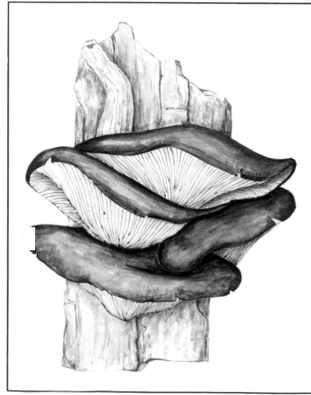

56

have a stalk covered in a sticky layer up to the false ring.

The species with brighter colours include. *Hygrophorus (= Camarophyllus) pratensis*, with a humped, reddish-tawny cap; the gills are decurrent, well-spaced and creamy, while the stalk tapers towards the base and is paler than the cap.

Brightly coloured, smaller hygrophoras include *H. conicus*, which, as one would expect, has a conical cap and is a sulphur-yellow colour

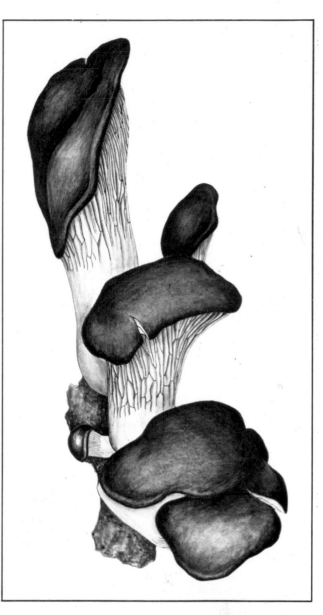

(Left) Hygrophorus hypothejus

(Below, far left) Oyster fungus, Pleurotus ostreatus, *an edible species*

(Below left) Melanoleuca vulgaris

(Right) Pleurotus columbinus, *sometimes regarded as a variety of* P. ostreatus

(Below) Lentinus tigrinus, *frequently found on old tree-stumps*

which blackens with age; *H. puniceus* also has a conical cap which is scarlet; *H. psittacinus* (= *Hygrocybe psittacina*), is slender, with a bell-shaped, sticky cap and a stalk tipped with green. All have yellowish gills, and a slender stalk of the same colour as the cap.

We come now to a group of white-spored agarics characterized by a particular shape, namely the *Pleurotus* species. These have virtually no stalk, and, if they do, it is curved and eccentric depending on the way in which the toadstool is inserted into the tree trunk on which it lives.

The most common species is *Pleurotus ostreatus*, the Oyster Fungus, with a wide cap which is rather shell-shaped and of a violet-brown colour. The gills are widely spaced and decurrent down the short stalk which is joined to one side of the cap. This is an edible toadstool when young, and is found on trees such as beech in late autumn and winter.

Pleurotus cornucopiae usually appears before *P. ostreatus*, and is found on elm, oak and other large deciduous trees. The cap is fleshy, rather wavy, and of a whitish colour which becomes fawn with age. The stalk is more distinct in this species, and the gills are strongly decurrent. The white flesh has a mealy smell.

Both *Lentinus lepideus* and *Lentinellus cochleatus* have central stalks, although they can be regarded as *Pleurotus* species. The first is quite common on old conifer stumps and on soft-wood such as telegraph poles and railway sleepers. The cap, though yellowish, is covered with brown scales, and the stalk is stout. The second species has very funnel-shaped caps and is found in clumps especially on beech stumps. Its gills are strongly decurrent, a pale ochre-red. The flesh has a pleasant smell of aniseed.

From those agarics with a convex or umbonate cap we pass to those whose cap, at least in the mature forms, is flattened or funnel-shaped. We can list at least three genera: *Paxillus, Russula* and *Lactarius*, all woodland toadstools; though there are many others with a sunken cap.

The first genus, *Paxillus*, is widely represented by *P. involutus*, common in summer under birch and in mixed woods generally. The specific name *involutus* refers to the inrolling of the cap margin. This charming toadstool is in various shades of brown, the gills being a yellowish-brown and becoming darker if bruised. The spores, too, are ochrish-brown. Possibly poisonous if eaten raw, this *Paxillus* is harmless when cooked, even though it is not very tasty.

The genus *Russula* is a large one, containing many species which are difficult to identify. We shall deal only with those species which are common in most types of wood and which are well defined. A great variety of colours is found in the russulas, even within individual species. Each species is also affected by age, the type of wood in

(*Above*) Paxillus involutus *is edible if cooked. Similar to the lactarii, it is an unusual shade of brown*

(*Left*) Russula cyanoxantha *is found in a wide variety of colours, two extremes of which are shown here*

which it grows, the light intensity and the amount of rainfall. They are generally characterized by brittle gills and granular flesh, without the milk found in *Lactarius* species; the cap is convex at first, becoming sunken, and the stalk is thick and slightly swollen at the base.

One of the commonest Russulas is *R. cyan-xantha*, which has a bluish-green or violet cap; this colour can be washed out by rain. It is an excellent toadstool to eat. The flesh is white but is tinted below the skin of the cap.

Russula virescens is also edible; it is thicker than the previous species and a little deformed. The colour of the cap is basically verdigris, spotted with polygonal tufts or scales. The cap cracks with age to reveal the white flesh. The stalk is white and tapers downwards. This is another russula which is very good to eat.

Not all the russulas are brightly coloured;

(Above) Russula albonigra, *and (right) stages of development of* Russula emetica, *the Sickener*

(Below) Russula lepida *ranges from scarlet and carmine to ochre and clear red*

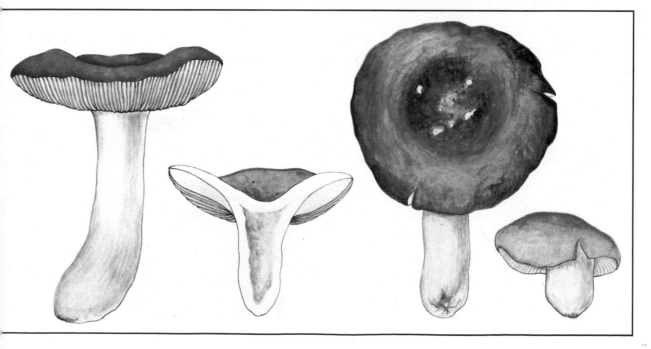

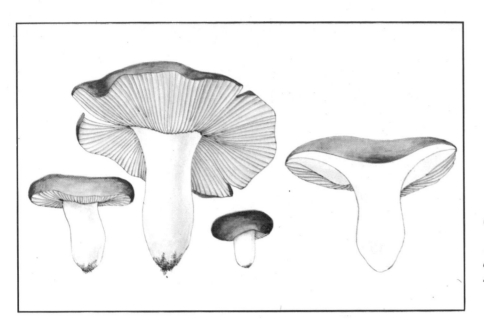

(Left) Russula rubra, *in various stages of development*

(Below left) Russula olivacea, *an edible species, is also variable in colour. Here, a red-brown form is shown with its cream-coloured gills*

R. delica, for example, is almost totally white, though spotted with brown. The name *delica* means 'without milk' or 'weaned', a reference to the fact that, although this species could be mistaken easily for a lactarius, it is in fact a russula. The fleshy cap quickly becomes funnel-shaped, having an inrolled margin and a velvety surface. This toadstool can be confused with *Lactarius vellereus,* but a very simple means of distinguishing them is the fact that *R. delica* usually has crumbs of soil or fragments of dead leaves attached to it, because of the way it grows.

The flesh of the russulas is generally permanently white, but in one or two cases the flesh will change colour if broken or bruised. *R. nigricans,* the Blackening Russula, is a good example. It has a large cap of 10–20 cm diameter, turning naturally from white to grey-brown and eventually black with the flesh itself turning from white to a reddish tint if bruised. The taste is bitter and it is, therefore, not pleasant to eat.

The predominant colour among the russulas is red; more than one hundred species have this colour! The task of distinguishing them, bearing in mind the variation within one species, can be enormous. Features such as smell and taste, the colour and shape of the spores and the colour of the stalk, therefore have to be used. For example the gills vary in colour from off-white to various shades of yellow, while the spores have varying surface-structure and shape. Of course, one needs a microscope to see the spore features, so the amateur may have difficulty.

One of the most common and striking russulas is the Sickener, *R. emetica,* which is poisonous and all too easily confused with the edible *R. lepida.* The former, however, has a peppery, bitter taste while the latter smells of menthol or cedar wood.

Russula fragilis also has a bitter taste; it is smaller than the Sickener and is extremely fragile, breaking up if touched. It smells like pear drops.

Mention must also be made of *R. sardonia* which, like *R. emetica,* has a peppery taste, and *R. xerampelina,* which has a smell like that of crab or lobster and is quite edible.

The most important russulas with a purple-red cap include *R. atropurpurea* and *R. olivacea.* The former can be recognized by its purple cap with blackish centre, the latter by colour rings on its cap, and its gills which are yellow when ripe.

Russula violeipes is unusual in having a yellowish or peach-coloured cap and a purple stalk. *R. amoena* is sometimes regarded as a separate species, being extremely variable in its colours.

(Right, and below right) examples of the colour forms of Russula aurata, *which varies in the colour of both its cap and gills*

(Below) Russula sardonia, *with its distinctive stalk*

which range from purple to green or yellow. The gills of both are dense, cream-white in colour, and the stalk is often the same colour as the cap, though it is sometimes white. The smell of both types is characteristically 'fruity'.

This brief account of such a large group must be concluded with two more inedible species; the stinking Russula *(R. foetens)* and the Geranium-scented Russula *(R. fellea)*. The first has a much larger cap measuring 6–15 cm, which is ochrish in colour, darker at the centre, and has a furrowed, papillate (see glossary) margin. The gills of this species are white, becoming ochrish; the stalk is short, whitish and hollow. This foul-smelling toadstool is usually found in mixed woods.

Russula fellea, however, lacks the cap-edge decoration of *R. foetens* and the gills eventually have the same ochrish colour as the cap, while the stalk is a paler colour and is less hollow than in *R. foetens*. The geranium smell of the flesh, however, is the easiest distinguishing feature.

We have already stressed the main difference betwcen the russulas and the lactarii, namely the presence of a milk or latex in the latter. This can be seen easily if the flesh or gills are broken. Of the lactarii, the most famous (and tasty) is the Saffron Milk Cap, *Lactarius deliciosus*, commonly found in coniferous woods. This is a large

toadstool with an orange-red cap, which is ringed in red, and turns greenish if damaged. The milk rapidly turns a carrot colour on exposure and if consumed can temporarily turn urine red.

Lactarius sanguifluus has blood-red milk. It is closely related to the previous species, though less common. White milk, becoming rapidly yellow in air, is typical of *L. chrysorrheus,* which is inedible, and has an ochrish cap that turns red. Both these species are widespread in Europe and N. America, but are not found in Britain.

The Peppery Milk Cap, *L. piperatus,* also has white milk but this does not change colour at all on contact with air. There are several lactarii which share this feature; this one is distinguished by its serrated, forked gills, which become yellow with age. In some countries, such as those in the Balkans, this toadstool is crushed for use as a pepper substitute.

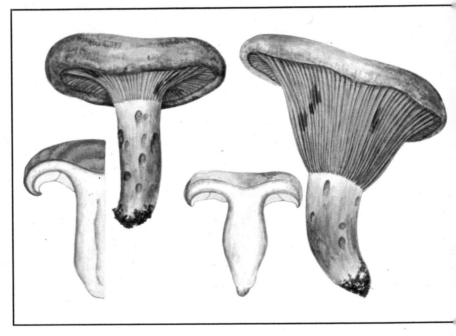

One of the largest lactarii is *L. vellereus,* the Fleecy Milk Cap, which has caps up to 20 cm in diameter. The cap is white and velvety, with, at maturity, an incurved edge and a sunken centre. It is rather acrid.

Ochrish gills are found in *L. scrobiculatus,* distinguished from the others by the pits dotted about the stalk, and by its white milk which becomes yellow on contact with air.

Two other lactarii deserve a mention: *Lactarius volemus* and the Woolly Milk Cap, *L. torminosus.* The former species is edible but mediocre; it has a golden-yellow or orange cap, with creamy white gills which turn ochrish, and become brown if bruised. The stalk is a little paler than the cap. The milk is abundant, white and mild. The second species, however, is robust and has its flesh-pink cap covered in a woolly down. The cap is also zoned with circular bands. This species is best avoided because of its bitter taste.

Another lactarius with a zoned cap is *L. aurantiacus,* which we can take to represent a group of very similar, orange-coloured species found particularly in coniferous woods. *L. quietus,* edible but of poor quality, is common during summer and autumn in oak woods. The cap is 4–10 cm across and becomes concave; the

(Opposite, top) Russula caerulea; *(centre)* Lactarius sanguifluus *at far left, and* L. deliciosus; *(bottom)* L. piperatus

(Below left) Lactarius torminosus; *(below right)* L. scrobiculatus; *(bottom left)* L. volemus; *(bottom right)* L. fuliginosus

gills are split at the base and are initially white, finally becoming the same as the cap (reddish-brown). The stalk is slender and lighter in colour than the cap. The flesh is white, while the normally white milk can turn cream and has a sweet smell. This toadstool is similar to *L. subdulcis*,

Two large specimens of Lactarius vellereus, *a very acrid and peppery species*

which is smaller and is red-pink. *L. subdulcis* is not zoned at all; it has reddish flesh and tastes at first sweet and then rather bitter. It is found in beech woods and is non-poisonous, though unpleasant.

A characteristic smell of curry is given off from the dry flesh of *L. camphoratus*; the cap is 3–6 cm in diameter, mainly brown-red in colour, plain convex and always with a small umbo.

Lactarius pyrogalus and *L. fuliginosus* both have grey-brown-green stalks, and are common in woods. The first has a zoned cap, while the second has not. They also have white gills which turn ochrish. Their flesh is acrid; the milk is white, but reddens in the case of *L. fuliginosus*.

A very large cap (10–25 cm) brown-olive in colour, characterizes *L. plumbeus (= L. turpis = L. necator),* occasionally found during summer and winter in birch woods; this is not poisonous but is rather acrid and regarded as inedible.

Basidiomycetes with pores

Not all *Basidiomycetes* have gills and some look very different from the typical mushrooms and toadstools. There is, however, one large group which has the outward appearance of a typical toadstool though it completely lacks gills. Instead of gills these toadstools have pores on the underside of the cap. These pores vary considerably in size and shape being round in some species, large and angular in others.

Although they share the presence of pores, these toadstools belong to two quite different groups: the *Boletinae* and the *Polyporales*. The former belong to the *Agaricales* but the latter form a quite distinct group. They can be distinguished by two main features – the boletes have a central stalk and the tube layer comes easily away from the rest of the cap; the polypores often have an eccentric stalk (see glossary) with the tubes adhering strongly to the flesh.

The boletes (generally the genus *Boletus*, but also including a number of other genera) have a solid and fleshy cap with an upper layer of flesh and a lower layer of tubes which end in the pores.

This group is very large indeed and quite variable. One identifying test which can be applied is the possible colour change that occurs when the flesh is bruised. In some the white flesh remains white; in others the yellow – or off-white – flesh may change to blue-green or even black.

Among those boletes which show such a colour change is the Devil's Boletus, *Boletus satanus*, a poisonous species which changes from whitish or cream to blue if bruised. This can be quite a large toadstool, having a grey-white cap suffused with olive-green. The pores are very small, at first yellow and becoming reddish-orange. The stalk is thick, grey at the base, yellow at the top and covered in a fine network of red veins.

Boletus rhodoxanthus can be confused with the previous species, having a distinctly yellow flesh that becomes blue and then red; the cap is at first cream, then reddish-grey, and the stalk is yellow

Boletes are characterized by having spongy tubes under the cap, lined with the hymenium (right). These tubes come away from the flesh easily and are open to the outside through small pores (far right)

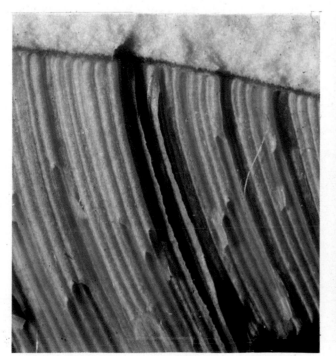
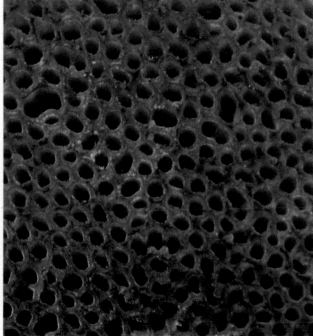

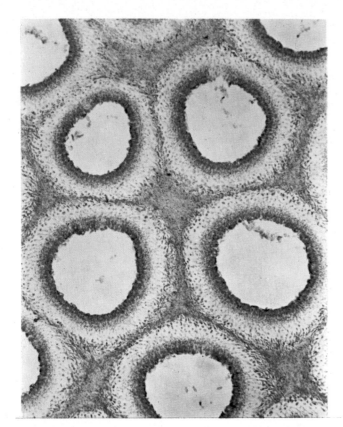

(Left) tubes of the Cep, Boletus edulis, under the microscope. The blue stain shows up the hymenium clearly as the layer which lines the tubes

(Below) the Devil's Boletus, Boletus satanas, a poisonous species with carmine pores and grey cap

overlaid with a red network. This species is toxic when raw, but is edible if cooked for a long time.

Three closely related boletes, none of which has been much used as food, are the Lurid Boletus *(B. luridus)*, having a network on the stalk; *Boletus erythropus* Fries *(= B. miniatoporus)*, having small red dots; and *B. erythropus* Persoon *(= B. queletii)*. The confusion between them has been increased by the fact that two authors (Fries and Persoon) have given the same specific name *(erythropus)* to these two separate but related species.

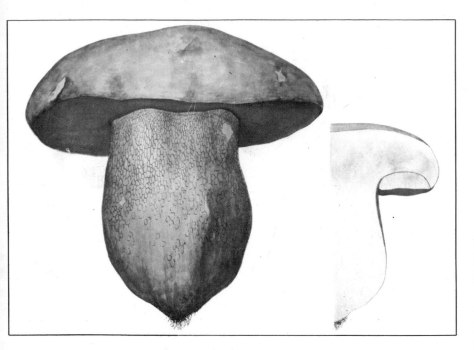

(Above) Boletus purpureus (= B. rhodoxanthus) *whose yellow flesh turns bluish when cut*

(Below) Boletus lupinus *has distinctive colours under the cap: the edge is yellow and the rest brilliant red*

These three boletes have pores which vary from yellow-ochre to orange-red and deep red in later life. *Boletus queletii* has a stalk with a definitely purple base and flesh.

We turn now to a group of boletes which is very common and harmless, even though the flesh turns blue or black on cooking. There are four common species in this group: *Boletus scaber (= Trachypus carpini = Leccinum griseum)*, with a grey-brown cap; *B. nigrescens (= Trachypus crocipodius = Leccinum crocipodius)*, with a brown cap which is often cracked; *B. rufus*

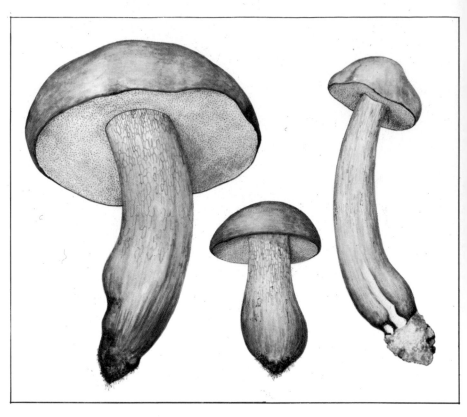

(= *Trachypus aurantiacus = L. aurantiacum*) with a red cap; and *B. duriusculus* (= *T. duriusculus = L. duriusculum*), smaller than the rest, and with a brown or smoky cap.

All these boletes are typified by a rough stalk covered in small scales, either brown or black according to the species.

Another important group of edible boletes is characterized by the fact that they are found in coniferous woods and have a very sticky cap. They also have a partial veil in the early stages of

(Above) three different specimens of Boletus luridus, *sharing the distinctive feature of a red network on the upper part of the stalk*

(Left and below) Boletus miniatoporus (=B. erythropus *Fries) which has numerous fire-red spots on the stalk*

(Right) Boletus queletii (= B. erythropus *Persoon) is very closely related to* B. miniatoporus *and has dense, granular, red spots on the stalk, which turns purple if broken*

their development, which leaves traces at the top of the stalk, like a ring.

One of the most important members of this group is *Boletus luteus (= Ixocomus = Suillus luteus)*, common in grassy woods; it has a chestnut-coloured cap which turns dark brown-red and is finely striped with darker lines. Its pores are small. The stalk changes from off-white to yellow, with the remains of the partial veil as a ring towards its top.

A second species, common in larch woods, is the Larch Boletus *(Boletus elegans = Ixocomus elegans = Suillus grevillei)*. This species is more slender than *B. luteus,* and has a yellow cap which turns reddish, and yellow pores. The stalk is the same colour as the cap, and displays the white or grey-brown remains of the veil. This is related to (and can be confused with) *Boletus flavus (= Ixocomus flavus = Suillus nueschii)*, which has cap, stalk and pores of lemon-yellow. The Sticky Boletus *(Boletus viscidus = Ixocomus viscidus = Suillus aeruginascens)* is similar, but

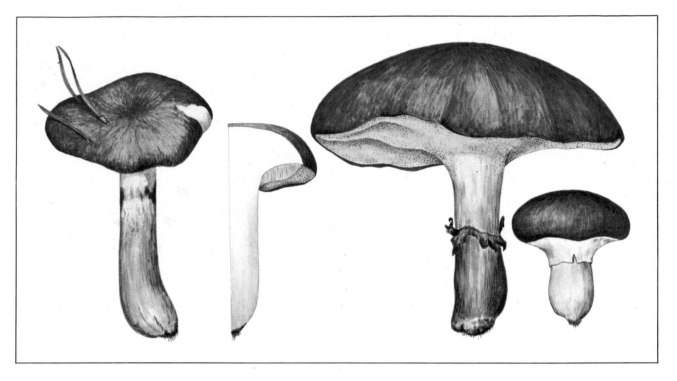

(Left) Boletus scaber (= Trachypus carpini)

(Below, far left) Boletus rufus (= B. aurantiacus), *a red species with granules*

(Below left) Boletus versipellis *with black stalk granules*

(Right) Boletus luteus, *with a dark ring on the stalk*

(Below) Boletus elegans, *common in larch woods*

has grey-brown tones and a much more sticky cap.

Another bolete with a sticky cap, but lacking any trace of a ring is *Boletus (= Suillus) granulatus,* which grows in coniferous woods, and has a red-brown cap, with yellow pores and stalk. The upper part of the stalk is distinguished by

granules. Similar granules are also found in *Boletus (= Suillus) placidus,* although they are more like small, red warts. Both the stalk and cap of the species, which is found in parks or pine plantations, are off-white in colour.

All these boletes are much sought after; they should be gathered in dry weather avoiding specimens which are very old. The caps should be skinned since the sticky skin is indigestible.

Less sought-after are *Boletus (= Ixocomus = Suillus) bovinus,* common in pine woods, especially on acid soil, and *Boletus (= Boletinus) cavipes.* The former has a sticky, reddish-ochre cap and a stalk which is slender and a little paler than the cap. The cap of the latter is not sticky but instead is covered in small, brown scales, and the yellow-green pores are large and angular. One notable feature of this second species is the hollow stalk which also has a trace of a veil at the top.

Lastly we come to the most famous, and edible, group of boletes, which include *B. edulis,* the Cep. This is often regarded as the most typical of the boletes, and is well-known for both its excellent and safe eating qualities and for the variety of colours found in its cap. These colours vary from ochre to semi-white and even brown. A form of the common Cep, which is sometimes regarded as a sub-species or variety, and, at other times, as a separate species *(B. reticulatus = B. aestivalis),* has a more pronounced network on the stalk.

It is quite easy to distinguish *Boletus aereus* from the Cep, by virtue of its sooty cap, and similarly *B. pinicola* with its copper-red cap, although it is regarded by some experts as a sub-species of the Cep *(B. edulis).*

Boletus pinicola has a fine, white network on the stalk, and a reddish tint to the flesh under the cap skin. All three of the last-named species, however, have permanently white flesh, though in *B. pinicola* the flesh of adult specimens turns slightly red. Furthermore, in some countries, all three species are eaten in a variety of forms (dried, fresh, in oil or vinegar, for example).

Another bolete easily confused with the Cep is *B. felleus* (= *Tylopilus felleus*), but it can be distinguished by virtue of its pinkish pores and its extremely bitter taste. In addition, the flesh is white, but becomes pinker on contact with air. Although obviously unpalatable because of its

There are many boletes with sticky caps to be found in larch woods. These five species can be distinguished by their colouring. (Top row, left to right) Boletus elegans, B. flavus, B. viscidus; *(bottom row)* B. bresadolae, *and* B. tridentinus *in different stages*

bitterness, this bolete is not actually poisonous.

One of the most distinctive and impressive colour changes found among the boletes is that shown by *Boletus* (= *Gyroporus*) *cyanescens*. Both flesh and tubes, but more especially the flesh, turn deep blue if bruised or cut. This is an edible and tasty fungus. The cap, 5–10 cm across,

(Above) Boletus bresadolae (=Ixocomus bresadolae)

(Above right) Boletus tridentinus

(Right) Boletus (=Boletinus) cavipes

(Above left) Boletus bovinus

(Above) Boletus placidus, *rather similar to* B. granulatus

(Left) Boletus pinicola

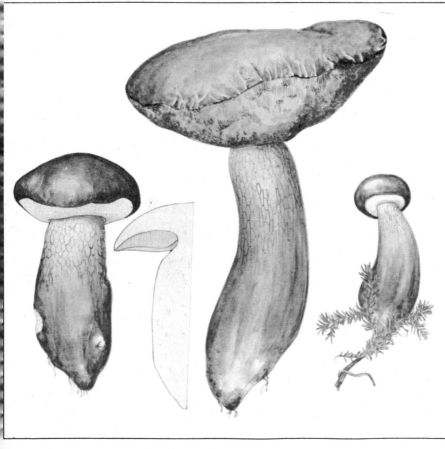

(*Above*) Boletus edulis, *the Cep*

(*Left*) Boletus felleus, *easily confused with the Cep. It can be distinguished by its bitter taste, its pink pores and its more definite network on the stalk*

is a pale ochre in colour, with fluffy scales on it. Small, white-yellowish pores and a hollow stalk are also features of this species. It is found during summer and autumn in acid, dry woodlands, especially among conifers such as spruce. There is a variety of it known as *lacteus* which is completely white, but still shows the same colour change.

The flesh of *B. calopus* also turns blue on bruising, but the colour to which it changes is not so deep and is more greenish. It is relatively common in a variety of woods, but is not eaten on account of its bitter taste. The cap is somewhat hemispherical at first, becoming convex and hairy, greyish or blue-brown in colour. The stalk is yellow at the top and carmine elsewhere, covered with a white network which helps to identify this bolete.

A common medium-size bolete (4–10 cm) is *Boletus* (=*Xerocomus*) *subtomentosus*. This

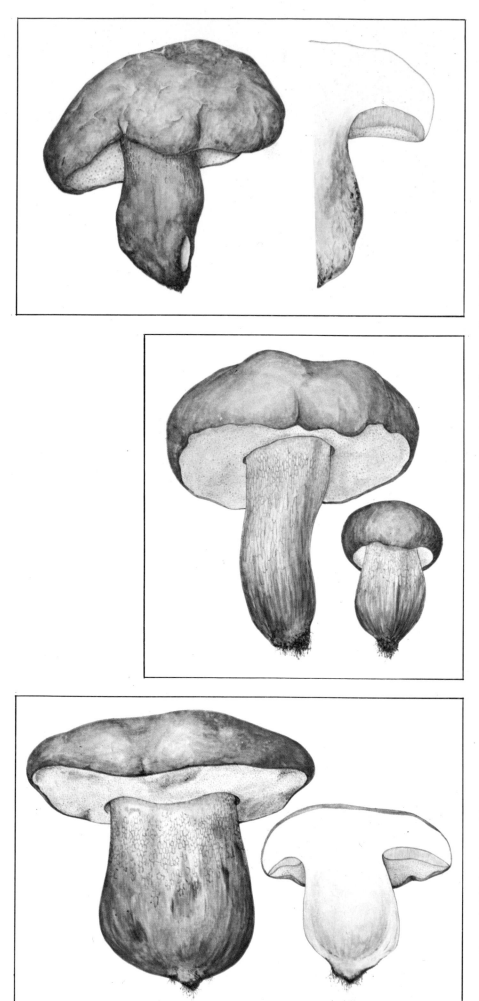

species is typified, as one would expect, by a tomentose or hairy cap, which is olive-brown in colour. The tubes are yellow, while the pores are angular and large. Its cylindrical stalk, slightly swollen at the middle, is yellowish and ribbed vertically. The flesh of this edible fungus is white or yellowish, but tinted brown under the skin.

B. chrysenteron is a slightly smaller bolete than *B. subtomentosus,* but has the same velvety appearance to the cap. The yellowish stalk is relatively slender for a bolete and tapers at the base. Edible but not particularly tasty, the flesh of this species is yellow and turns bluish on exposure to air. It is common in all sorts of woods.

Boletus (= Xerocomus) badius also has the same velvety texture as *B. subtomentosus.* The cap is 7–15 cm in diameter and bay-brown in colour (hence its specific name), while the tubes and the small, angular pores are yellow, though the pores turn greenish if bruised. The stalk is slender, yellow-ochre to brown in colour, and its pale yellow flesh, turns green-blue in the air. This species is most commonly found under conifers in summer and autumn and is quite edible.

This account of the boletes is best concluded by mentioning two small and interesting species. The first is *Boletus (= Suillus = Ixocomus) piperatus,* commonly found in pine woods. It has a peppery taste, and consequently is not too good to eat. The cap, 2–5 cm in diameter, is yellow-brown, and the large, angular pores are terracotta or red. The stalk is slender, yellow-ochre, golden at the base, while the flesh is sulphur-yellow.

The second species is interesting in that it is parasitic on *Scleroderma aurantium* (Common Earth-ball). Not surprisingly, it is named *Boletus (= Xerocomus) parasiticus.* The cap is ochre-brown, with large, yellow pores, the stalk is yellow-ochre and curved. In spite of its parasitic habit it is considered edible, though inferior in taste.

Modern systems of classification are, certainly in the case of toadstools, a great improvement on the old ones. This is reflected most clearly in the large number of changes in genera, although this is, unfortunately, very confusing to the layman.

Much of this improvement is quite recent and without doubt it will continue for some time to come. One of the most significant changes is the recognition that the boletes and the polypores are quite separate; there are many features which separate them, but the most obvious, and hence most useful from the point of view of recognizing them in the field, is that the boletes have a definite stalk which is joined centrally on to the cap, while the polypores either have no stalk at all, or a short one which is joined to one side of the cap.

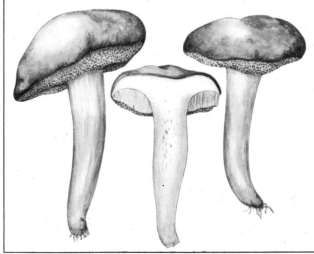

(Above) Boletus (=Ixocomus) variegatus

(Opposite, top) Boletus calopus (=B. pachypus) *which has a reddish or pink stalk overlaid by a network*

(Opposite, centre) Boletus appendiculatus, *an edible species whose stalk has a network on a yellow background*

(Opposite, bottom) Boletus regius, *sometimes considered a variety of* B. appendiculatus

(Right) Boletus subtomentosus, *which is edible*

(Below) Boletus parasiticus, *living on* Scleroderma aurantium, *and (below right)* B. piperatus

There are numerous examples of polypores without a stalk, where the cap (if one can still call it that) is joined directly on to the trunk or stump on which it is growing. This results in a 'shelf' or 'bracket', which has obviously led to the popular names for these fungi. One must not forget, however, that there are polypores which live on soil and have a stalk on one side of the cap.

Although many polypores are edible in the young state, generally speaking the flesh is too tough, or even 'woody', to be eaten.

Closely related to the polypore family *(Poly-poraceae)* are the *Fistulinaceae,* distinguished from the former by having separate tubes. The best-known member of this family is the Beefsteak Fungus *(Fistulina hepatica)* which is large and often has a blood-red colour. Some people use it in cookery for the delicious flavour it imparts to food. It is a true shelf or bracket fungus and is found especially on the trunks of oak or chestnut. The upper surface of the cap becomes sticky with

age, and the pores are yellowish and turn brown-red if touched. The flesh not only looks like fresh meat but also has the same feel to it.

Returning to the polypore family itself, one of the commonest and most striking species is *Polyporus (= Polyporellus) squamosus,* from 10–30 cm in diameter, with the hollowed, upper surface ochre-yellow and covered in many large, brown and feathery scales. The lower surface is white and covered in pores, while the stalk is rather short and inserted in one side of the cap. This is a widespread species found on many types of tree, especially elm, and it is found throughout summer and autumn. It is considered edible while young.

Another large polypore is *Polyporus frondosus (= P. intybaceus = Grifola frondosa),* which has complex brackets made up of many small ones joined together. It grows on many trees, especially oak, and is found in autumn. Each cap is grey-brown above and white below. It is sometimes

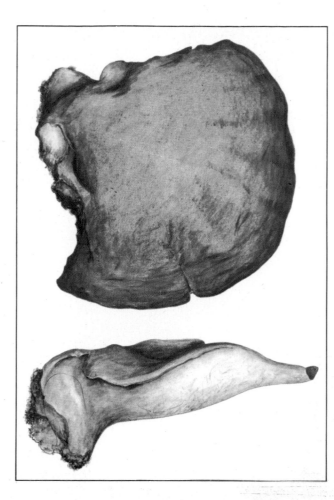

(*Above*) *Beefsteak Fungus*, Fistulina hepatica

(*Far left*) *a fine example of the Bay Boletus*,
B. badius, *and (left)* Strobilomyces floccopus,
easily identified by the very large scales on the cap

(*Below, and below right*) Polyporus pes-caprae
(= P. scobinaceus); *the cap is smothered in dark
brown scales, while the stalk is attached to one side*

eaten. Even larger is *Polyporus giganteus (= Grifola gigantea)*, which can grow up to 1 m across and is commonly 50 or 60 cm. Like the previous species, several caps occur on the same specimen; the caps are brown above and white below. The flesh is somewhat fibrous and therefore not worth eating.

Easily recognized because of its sulphur-yellow pores and orange or light-coloured surfaces is *Polyporus sulphureus (= Grifola sulphurea)*. This polypore attacks a wide range of trees, causing a lot of decay, especially in oak. The large brackets (30–40 cm) arise from a short stalk. The flesh is slightly acid but can be eaten when young.

Among the species of polypore which grow in soil is *Polyporus (= Polystictis = Coltrichia) perennis*, which has a leathery, fan-shaped and funnelled cap narrowing into the stalk. This dark brown cap is zoned with lighter bands and the pores are small and grey, also becoming brown. Quite a common species in woods and on heaths, particularly on burnt soil, this fungus can be found throughout the year.

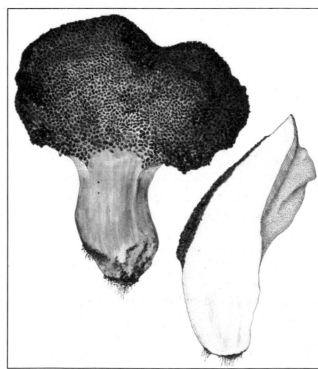

(Above left)
Polyporus cristatus,
an edible species with
a lobed cap

(Left) Polyporus
(=Polyporellus)
squamosus, *which is*
large and found on
tree trunks, is edible
when young

80

(Above and above right) Polyporus (= Polypilus) frondosus, *an edible species which can grow very large. The cap is split into many brown or grey frond-like parts*

(Below, and right) two pictures of a shelf fungus, Polyporus sulphureus

Also on soil at the base of rotting trees is the Shining Ganoderma, *Ganoderma lucidum*, with its rounded, shining stalk, which appears most odd as the fungus is growing (see photograph, top left on page 82). This stalk bears a kidney-shaped cap which is similarly purple-red or chestnut in colour.

The remaining two species which we shall mention are both found on trees: *Piptoporus betulinus* and *Polyporus versicolor*.

The former, Birch Polypore, is obviously found on birch *(Betula)* and has shell-shaped caps

81

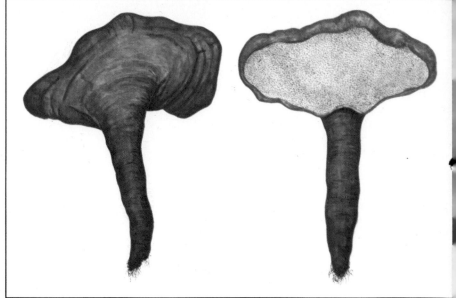

which are brown above and white beneath. The flesh is corky. It is commonly found on dead or dying birch trees, where it not only causes their death but continues to digest them once they are dead.

The latter species, also known as *Trametes versicolor,* is responsible for much decay of felled timber. The brackets are zoned, with the edge a much lighter colour than the rest, which may be grey, greenish-brown or black. They frequently occur in large, tiered masses.

(Top, far left and above) Ganoderma lucidum *in young and mature forms*

(Centre) Piptoporus betulinus, *found on birch trees*

(Bottom left) the small Polyporus perennis; *(below)* P. versicolor

Other Basidiomycetes

Other than toadstools with gills or pores, there also exists in the *Basidiomycetes* various other odd, small groups well worth attention. These additional groups include the chanterelles, the tooth fungi, club fungi, puff-balls and earth-balls.

Of the chanterelles, the most common and famous is probably the true Chanterelle, *Cantharellus cibarius,* rather a small fungus never larger than 7–8 cm in height. Its colour is a distinctive yellow all over and the cap quickly sinks to its characteristic shape with a lobed, wavy edge. The simple 'gills' are forked and decurrent down the stalk. The flesh is also yellow and has the smell of apricots – a feature which

distinguishes it from the False Chanterelle, *Hygrophoropsis aurantiacus.* This toadstool is quite common in many woods during autumn and is often collected because of its excellent taste.

There are several varieties of the Chanterelle named according to the cap colour: white in var. *alba* and orange in var. *friesii.* Sometimes placed with the white-spored agarics, the chanterelles are probably best regarded as primitive gill fungi worthy of a completely separate group.

Related species are *Cantharellus cinereus,* which is entirely greyish and somewhat smaller, and *C. infundibuliformis (= C. tubaeformis)* which has a

Group of Chanterelles, Cantharellus cibarius, *highly prized as a food*

(Above) two views of Hydnum (=Sarcodon) imbricatum, *a tooth fungus with large brown scales*

(Above, far left) Horn of Plenty, Craterellus cornucopioides

(Above left) teeth of Hydnum repandum *under a microscope, showing the darkly stained hymenium*

(Left) the Common Hydnum, Hydnum repandum, *enlarged to show the distinctive spines*

yellow stalk and grey-brown cap. Both are edible.

The Horn of Plenty, *Craterellus cornucopioides,* is also known as the *trompette des morts* in France, on account of its unwholesome appearance. It is, in fact, quite edible and is widely used as a flavouring. The overall outline is similar to that of the chanterelles, but it is dark grey in colour, leading to brown inside and black outside. There are no traces of gills, merely folds on the fertile layer, which is outside and underneath the cap.

In the tooth fungi, the fertile layer is borne on the surface of the teeth found on the underside of the cap. One of the most frequent species is *Hydnum repandum,* the Common Hydnum, which is edible, though bitter, and must be boiled before eating. The fleshy cap is convex, irregularly lobed, and of a yellow-ochre colour tending to orange. Underneath, the pale teeth are crowded down part of the stalk. The stalk itself is short and

eccentric, being either whitish or the same colour as the cap.

The family of the tooth fungi (the *Hydnaceae*) contains many species formerly referred to the genus *Hydnum* but now put in separate genera. One of these is *Sarcodon (=Hydnum) imbricatum.* It has a fleshy, concave cap covered in scales darker than the brown background. The teeth are at first white but become brown, like the cap. The bitter taste of the white flesh does not prevent this species from being popularly eaten.

The club or coral fungi are characterized by their very unusual shape which may be that of a club, hand or coral. One of the most common is *Clavaria (=Ramaria) botrytis,* which can be up to 30 cm broad and 15 cm high. Starting off from a wide, single stalk, the fruiting body branches repeatedly, like a cauliflower, to produce a coral-like structure which is red or lilac at the top. The flesh is permanently white.

Many of these fungi have a bitter taste, and in one case this is not even removed by boiling. Among the many species the most common are *Clavaria (=Ramaria) formosa,* a pinkish and poisonous form, whose tips are tinged yellow; and *C. flava,* which is a bright, sulphur-yellow.

A much simpler type is found in *Clavaria pistillaris,* a truly club-shaped species found in woods. The club is yellow-ochre and can grow up to 30 cm high, though it is usually very much smaller. It is edible.

Another diverse and interesting group includes the puff-balls, of the genus *Lycoperdon*, and their relatives the earth-balls, *Scleroderma* species. In fact, puff-balls are now placed in more than one genus; those species which simply burst at the top to release spores are put in the genus *Calvatia*.

Out of all the puff-balls the largest is *Calvatia gigantea*. This species can quite commonly reach 40 cm in diameter, and has been recorded up to 1 metre. It is found during summer and autumn in fields and pastures, and is delicious to eat when young (in fact, all puff-balls are edible when young). The outside layer of the puff-ball is called the peridium, while the inner 'gleba' is at first white and firm, later becoming a brown, powdery mass of spores.

(Above left) Clavaria botrytis; *(above)* Clavaria pistillaris. *Both are club or coral fungi*

(Left) Clavaria cristata, *slightly enlarged, a rather insignificant species which may be eaten raw*

(Right) Calocera (= Clavaria) viscosa, *much enlarged, not toxic but of no nutritional value*

One of the commonest puff-balls is *Lycoperdon gemmatum* (= *L. perlatum*), 2–6 cm across, turning from white to ochre and covered in small, pointed warts. This is a species found in woods during summer and autumn. The peridium is pear-shaped.

The puff-balls must not be confused with the earth-balls, such as *Scleroderma aurantium* (= *S. vulgare*), which is completely spherical and yellow, covered in small warts. The gleba eventually turns black, and the peridium, or skin, is thick. In quantity, this earth-ball is poisonous but it can still be used in place of truffles in various foodstuffs. The use of a microscope can distinguish between them, since the truffles belong to the *Ascomycetes* and have quite different spores.

The stinkhorns are another group of *Gastero-*

mycetes, including *Phallus* (= *Ithyphallus*) *impudicus* and *Clathrus cancellatus,* both of which are characterized by the appalling smell of rotten meat which they produce. The true Stinkhorn (*Phallus*) produces its gleba on a long stalk which grows extremely rapidly. The olive-green gleba is soon exposed and becomes liquid, emitting its strong smell to attract flies which will distribute the spores. The stalk is white or reddish, cylindrical and pitted. In the very young state, this fungus can be found underground as a white 'egg'. *Clathrus cancellatus* produces a latticed gleba without a stalk.

Mutinus caninus, the Dog's Stinkhorn, is more streamlined than the true Stinkhorn and has a buff or reddish stalk tipped with the black mass of spores.

(Above) Sparassis crispa *(also known as* Clavaria crispa *and* Helvella ramosa) *is edible when young*

(Top) Lycoperdon pyriforme

(Centre)
Lycoperdon perlatum (= L. gemmatum), *light in colour, and* Lycoperdon molle, *which is darker*

(Right) Bovista plumbea

Abridged classification of the larger fungi

Basidiomycetes (spores formed in basidia) See pages 27–92	*Heterobasidiomycetes* (forked basidia)	jelly fungi (e.g. *Auricularia* species)
	Homobasidiomycetes (simple basidia)	
	1 *Gasteromycetes* (no hymenium)	puff-balls (e.g. *Lycoperdon* species) earth-balls (e.g. *Scleroderma* species) stinkhorns (e.g. *Phallus* species)
	2 *Hymenomycetes* (hymenium present)	agarics (e.g. *Amanita* species) boletes (e.g. *Boletus* species) polypores (e.g. *Polyporus* species) tooth fungi (e.g. *Hydnum* species) coral fungi (e.g. *Clavaria* species) dry rots (e.g. *Serpula* species)
Ascomycetes (spores formed in asci) See pages 93–100	*Discomycetes* (disc fungi)	cup fungi (e.g. *Peziza* species) earth fungi (e.g. *Geoglossum* species) morels and lorchels (e.g. *Morchella* species)
	Tuberales (underground)	truffles (e.g. *Tuber* species)

The earth-stars are yet another group, quickly recognized by the way in which the peridium splits open. These species belong to *Geastrum* (= *Geaster* = *Astraeus*). They are not worth eating but are nevertheless very interesting. The peridium has two layers, the outer one splits into 6–10 parts and folds back, exposing the inner layer, from which the spores are released through a pore or after splitting. These flaps open and close according to the humidity. There are many types found world-wide, but they are not common.

(Left) group of earth-balls, Scleroderma aurantium (= S. vulgare), *inedible because the gleba becomes violet-black and slimy. The top of the fruiting body opens to release spores (below).*

(Above right and right) young specimens of Phallus (= Ithyphallus) impudicus; *the lower example shows an 'egg' cut lengthways to demonstrate various parts.* Other Basidiomycetes *are shown on the next page*

Edible Ascomycetes

The *Ascomycetes,* like the *Basidiomycetes,* are a very large group (see classification table on page 90), but they have far fewer types which are edible. Among the edible species there are three main types: the morels and false morels; the cup fungi; and the truffles. The first two groups are found above ground, on soil, or sticks and even on plaster, while the truffles are exclusively subterranean species.

The true morels belong mainly to the genus *Morchella,* and are found in spring in woods and under hedges where the soil is rich. The feature which allows the morels to be recognized at once is their conical, honeycombed cap (mitre) which sits on a hollow, more or less cylindrical stalk.

One of the largest, and possibly the best-known, species is *Morchella esculenta,* widely eaten for its excellent flavour. Some people are upset to varying extents after eating it and only small amounts should be consumed at first. The size is

(Below left) cap of a morel (Morchella *species) seen in stained section under a microscope. The entire outer surface is lined with darkly staining hymenium*

(Below) greatly enlarged, stained portion of hymenium from a morel. The cylindrical asci containing the eight spores can be clearly seen

(Left) fully-grown Phallus impudicus

(Top left) Mutinus caninus

(Centre left) Clathrus cancellatus, *surely one of the most intriguing fungi in existence*

(Bottom left) Common Earth Star, Geaster (=Geastrum) rufescens, *has a complex fruiting body in which the outer layer splits and folds backwards as it dries. The spores are released through a hole in the top of the inner layers*

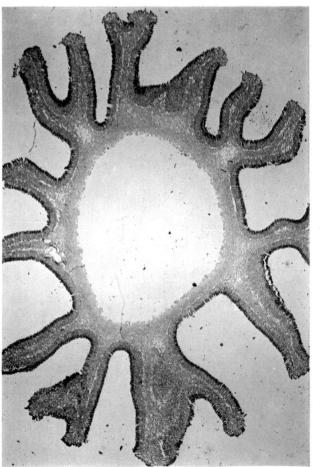

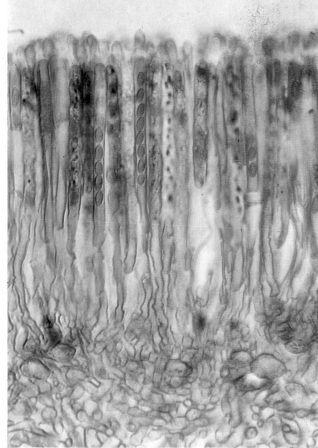

93

(Right) Mitrophora hybrida; *(below right)* Mitrophora semi-libera. *The second species is distinguished by having a more strongly ridged and granular stalk*

(Above left) Common morel, Morchella esculenta (= M. rotunda)

(Left) Morchella vulgaris

rather variable, but it can grow to 24 cm in
height. The yellow-brown cap has large, rather
regular pits on its surface, while the stalk is fat,
smooth and brittle. Two varieties are fairly easily
recognized: variety *rotunda* with a voluminous
and rounded head, and variety *esculenta* with a
thickened and conical head.

Rather similar to *Morchella esculenta* is *M.
vulgaris*; it is smaller and has a dark grey cap
with irregular-sided pits; the stalk is a much
lighter colour than that of *M. esculenta*.

Another species, *Morchella conica,* has a
conical cap, with the dark, olive-brown pits in
more or less definite rows. The top of the stalk is
virtually as wide as the base of the cap, and the
whole stalk is mealy and white to yellow-brown.
Like the other species it is edible, and is found on
rich soil in copses and conifer plantations.

Related to *Morchella* are *Mitrophora, Verpa*
and *Gyromitra. Mitrophora hybrida,* like other
Mitrophora species, has the cap partly free from
the stalk. In *Morchella,* as we have seen, cap and
stalk are completely united. In this species the cap
is small in relation to the long, mealy stalk, and is
dark brown-grey with relatively few ridges. The
closely related *Mitrophora semi-libera* has a
ridged stalk, but otherwise there is little to
distinguish them. Both can be eaten.

Verpa species have the cap completely free

(Above) cup fungus, Peziza repanda; the hymenium is the brown layer lining the cup

(Above left) Helvella crispa; (left) Helvella monachella. Both are edible, though inferior to morels

from the stalk, except, of course, at the very centre. The cap is almost smooth, having very few wrinkles, and the long, thin, stalk is ringed in scales.

Any specimen with a mop-like head and brain-like convolutions on a hollow, short stalk is likely to be *Gyromitra esculenta,* which, in spite of its name, is not safely edible. It contains helvellic acid, which is not always destroyed by cooking. The colour of the cap is red-brown, while that of the stalk is whitish. This species is found on sandy soils, particularly near conifers.

The false morels, or lorchels, belong to the genus *Helvella.* They can be recognized by the saddle-shaped or cup-shaped head which looks untidy, as though parts have been eaten away. Since they mainly fruit in summer and autumn, they are not really likely to be confused with the true morels, which appear in spring. They are all poisonous when raw, and are not completely safe when cooked: they are best avoided.

Helvella crispa grows up to 10 cm high with a whitish, saddle-shaped cap. The stalk is deeply grooved and white. It is found on rich soil among grass by paths or in woods. A second species, *H. lacunosa,* is very similar to *H. crispa,* but the cap is more irregularly lobed and is black or brown-black. The stalk is slightly lighter than the cap and is deeply grooved vertically. This is a woodland species, being found particularly on burnt soil.

The cup fungi are an extremely large group of *Ascomycetes,* but we shall deal only with the genus *Peziza* and its close relatives such as *Sarcoscypha.* Generally small fungi with a typical cup-like structure which either sits on the ground or on a short and slender stalk, these *Ascomycetes* have the fertile layer *inside* the cup rather than underneath it. There are many edible species belonging to this group, but their appearance and colour, together with their elastic or gelatinous flesh, does not exactly whet the appetite.

The Orange Peel Fungus, *Peziza aurantia,* is one of the largest and most striking of the cup fungi, being up to 12 cm in diameter. As one would expect, it is a vivid orange or scarlet inside the cup, which is irregularly lobed. It is fragile and a pale orange-white on the outside.

Peziza (= Sarcoscypha) coccinea, the Scarlet Elf Cup, is a definite scarlet colour within its medium-size cup (2–6 cm). This species is found not on soil, like *P. aurantia,* but on decaying twigs and branches, being borne on short stalks. Another elf cup is *Peziza venosa,* the Scented Elf

Cup, so called because of its strong, nitrous smell. The cups of this species are brown inside, the outside being whitish.

One of the species with ear-shaped cups is *Peziza (=Otidea) onotica*. It is a yellowish colour and grows in small groups on the ground in woods, particularly oak woods. The height is usually 10 cm but this also includes the short stalk characteristic of this species.

Peziza (=Aleuria) vesiculosa, *another cup fungus common on soils in autumn. Despite its unattractive appearance, it is edible*

Toadstools and shelf fungi which kill trees	
Genus/species	**Tree attacked**
Armillaria mellea	ash, firs, Douglas fir, hemlocks, oaks, pines, poplars, walnut
Collybia velutipes	lime/basswood
Corticium species	firs, spruces
Fistulina hepatica	chestnut, oaks
Fomes species	ash, beech, fir, Douglas fir, hemlocks, junipers, larches, maple, oaks, pines, poplars, willows
Ganoderma species	hemlocks
Pholiota squarrosa	birch
Polyporus species	ash, beech, chestnut, cypress, fir, hemlocks, maple, oaks, pines, spruces, willows
Sparassis radicata	Douglas fir, larches, pines, spruces
Stereum species	birch, firs, maple, oaks

Edible Ascomycetes: truffles

There is a tremendous amount of folklore attached to the truffles, which, coupled with their high cost, lends them a popular interest and respectability not matched by their appearance and habitat. They grow some distance underground in woods and are extremely difficult to locate without the help of a trained pig or dog.

Occasionally a man can find the scent himself without assistance from animals but this is rare. The truly experienced truffle-hunter, however, will know of other signs which can lead him to his valuable quarry. Truffles which are forming near the surface will often crack it, thus giving an indication of their position. There are also several species of flies which live on them and a colony of truffles will, in the morning or evening, be surrounded by columns of these flies which also assist the hunter.

All the species valued as food belong to the genus *Tuber*; the usual commercial species is *T. melanosporum*. The fruiting body is rounded and black or reddish-black and covered in many-sided warts. The flesh is compact, red-black or violet, with grey or white veins. They are found in

Black Truffle, Tuber melanosporum, *enlarged to show the characteristic surface features*

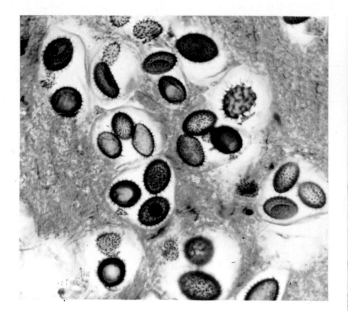

(Above) part of the flesh (gleba) of Tuber melanosporum, *stained to show the asci containing spores*

(Right and below) Tuber magnatum, *seen entire and sectioned. The gleba is characteristically mottled*

calcareous soil in oak woods, maturing during autumn and winter. Because of the obvious link between the planting of trees (particularly oak) and the growth of truffles, reforestation has been undertaken to yield better crops.

Another commercially important species is *T. magnatum*, which is outwardly grey or clay-coloured; internally the flesh is grey-brown or bistre-grey, with whitish veins of varying size which fuse and split in a very irregular pattern. The spores are large, oval and rough-coated. The flesh produces a pleasant smell. This species is found in a variety of woods. Gathering takes place during summer and autumn.

Tuber aestivum (= T. nigrum) is generally smaller than the preceding species, and is a brown-black colour with relatively large, distinct polygonal warts. The flesh is dark brown, with white veins. Although less strong than that of the other species, the smell of *T. aestivum* is very pleasant. Found in calcareous soil, mainly with beech, this truffle is collected in summer.

Other genera of truffles include *Elaphomyces*, *Balsamia* and *Terfezia,* containing some poisonous species. *Terfezia leonis* is a small species found in warm countries.

Cultivated mushrooms and toadstools

The possibility obviously exists that many species of fungi can be cultivated, particularly those which naturally live on a rich medium such as manure, since this can be easily obtained for cultivation. Edible toadstools with rather specialized requirements for growth are clearly much more difficult to grow.

Among microscopic fungi there are nowadays many examples of cultivation for man's use; in wine and beer fermentation and in making bread. There are also many moulds which provide antibiotics and are grown on a vast scale for this purpose. Similar moulds are involved in making cheese: the penicilliums, for example, are not only important for antibiotics but for imparting the special flavour and taste to Gorgonzola cheese *(Penicillium weidermanni var. fuscum = P. gorgonzolae)*, and to Neufchâtel, Coulommiers, Camembert and Brie cheeses *(P. biourgei, P. camemberti)*.

Usually, however, when thinking of cultivated fungi, it is mushrooms which come to mind. In fact, this is true in most developed countries, so widely are mushrooms grown.

(Below) Agrocybe cylindracea *(= Pholiota aegerita), an edible toadstool which is found on poplars and willows and can be cultivated on poplar trunks covered in soil*

Only those species of proven harmlessness and worth are used. They are grown nowadays in enormous quantity, not only for local fresh consumption, but for far-away markets and for the canning and dried-food industries. The way they are grown ensures continuous production unaffected by season, unlike wild mushrooms.

The nearest wild relative to the cultivated mushroom is thought by some specialists to be the Field Mushroom, *Agaricus campestris*. At first sight it certainly appears to be similar. Occasionally, one may also find references to *Agaricus bisporus*, which is obviously closer to the cultivated type *(A. bisporus* variety *albida)*.

Many authorities accept the latter as the true wild ancestor. Certainly, the usual mushroom of commerce has been cultivated for a very long time, continually being selected for better strains. The French were apparently the first to cultivate the mushroom, during the 18th century, since in 1707 the famous botanist, de Tournefort, described the way in which it was produced. Only since 1800, however, has the mushroom been cultivated on a commercial scale and the original techniques of the French have been improved continuously, adding also to the general knowledge of fungi.

The traditional compost in which mushrooms are grown is well-rotted horse manure mixed with straw and fine sand, together with some lime which increases its water-holding and aerating properties.

Originally, in the 'French' system, the compost was piled in heaps outdoors, and latterly in caves, producing mushrooms for two or three years. Other countries have since favoured different systems, sterilizing the compost in a variety of ways and inoculating it with chosen 'spawn' (blocks of mycelium) under the right conditions. Mushroom growing has therefore been transformed from an uncertain art to a

Pholiota squarrosa, *an autumn species which may be cultivated. It is edible, but a little indigestible*

Pholiota
(= Kuehneromyces)
mutabilis, *found on
old trunks*

(Below right)
Pholiota spectabilis,
edible but suspect

(Right) Armillaria mellea, *the Honey Fungus. Both this species, and* Pholiota spectabilis – *although slightly suspect – could possibly be cultivated*

105

precise science. Mushrooms do not need to be grown in the dark, but they need the right humidity and temperature, together with the correct sort of compost, packed not too tightly. In fact they can be grown perfectly well in greenhouses or sheds, but growing them underground in caves achieves more constant conditions so that continuous cropping can be achieved. The compost is also nowadays packed in trays which are stacked on top of each other. Even the original compost has changed considerably; people have experimented with all sorts of compost materials: maize, sawdust, liquorice roots and household refuse, for example. These have various chemicals such as calcium nitrate, ammonium nitrate or urea added to them.

Probably the greatest progress in producing large quantities of mushrooms has been made in the culturing of the spawn which is used for inoculating the compost. The original mushroom growers relied on the mushrooms 'seeding' the compost beds themselves, or on inserting pieces of mushroom into the compost. This was a rather hit-or-miss affair, naturally. Various early attempts to produce spawn from mushroom spores were also unreliable. Eventually, however, due to a great deal of experimentation, the methods of successful spawn production were discovered. Today, spawn production is very sophisticated, and includes means for ensuring pure strains and preventing other strains from infecting the compost to be used.

It takes about one month for the inoculated compost to produce the very small, white buttons that eventually form mushrooms, and about four to five months for the process of growth to be completed.

The artificial growing of mushrooms is only made possible by the fact that they live on decaying matter (that is to say they are saprophytic) and not in association with other living things either symbiotically or as a parasite. One may hazard a guess that other saprophytic toadstools could be grown commercially in the same way. Besides other species of *Agaricus,* possibilities include species of the genera *Volvaria* and *Coprinus,*

Morchella, Tricholoma, Pleurotus and *Lepiota*.

The Honey Fungus, *Armillaria mellea,* and *Pholiota aegerita* (= *Agrocybe cylindracea*) are both cultivated in some places on beds of rotting wood. Other species are occasionally cultivated in various parts of the world.

Toadstools such as the Cep, for example, cannot yet be cultivated because of their natural association with living trees, but the time will probably come when even this is possible. Work has also been in progress for some time on the possibility of cultivating truffles. If all these efforts are eventually commercially viable, the variety of mushrooms and toadstools available for eating will obviously be greatly increased.

(Above) one of the cultivated mushrooms, Agaricus hortensis *(slightly enlarged)*

(Right) colonies of the mould Penicillium notatum, *which provides penicillin*

Toadstools as food

Like most other products of the earth, toadstools and their relatives have interested man since prehistoric times; yet in the absence of definite knowledge we presume that men were unable to cultivate and breed them. What is certain, however, is that during the Greek and Roman times, toadstools were used as a food. It appears certain that Caesar's Amanita, *Amanita caesarea,* owes its name to the fact that it was a food of which Julius Caesar highly approved.

The writers of each age have written more or less exhaustively on the gastronomic delights of fungi, but the most authoritative evidence is in old, famous recipes, in which toadstools figure prominently. They have, at various times and places, come to be known as 'Poor Man's Meat', a reference to the fact that peasants have for centuries gathered toadstools wherever they could be found and used them as a substitute for meat, which the peasant could not afford.

Unfortunately, through the ages, the collection of toadstools has been a somewhat haphazard operation without any regard for common sense or respect for nature. Most collectors have had no knowledge of biology, especially mycology, whether in theory or in practice; they have simply gathered just the few species which they have definitely known to be edible, trampling and

(Left) Cep, Boletus edulis, *one of the most widely eaten toadstools*

(Above) Boletus pinicola; *(below)* Amanita caesarea. *Both are excellent foods, and can be used in a variety of ways: fresh, cooked or preserved*

destroying all other types, even quite edible ones, before they have had a chance to open out and release their spores. The consequence of this is obvious; the balance of nature becomes upset, however imperceptibly, and, under enough collecting pressure a great many species will become locally extinct. In other cases, the indiscriminate collectors have gathered more or less all the toadstools they have encountered, without any regard for their edibility or their state. The net result has been the same; the local toadstool flora has suffered, and of course this has meant less food for the local population.

At the same time, inexpert collection, without any form of control, has inevitably meant that many inedible or even poisonous species were consumed. One can only assume that this is one of the ways in which people learned, if they survived, which species were edible!

However, toadstools are a useful part of the diet, providing variety in taste, texture and nutrient. The popular name of 'Poor Man's Meat' implies a high protein content which they do not have. Fungi, like other fresh vegetables, contain many useful substances, although they are 78–92 per cent water. The most important structural substance is mycocellulose (a special type of cellulose) and fungal chitin (similar to the hard substance found in animal shells). Besides the usual organic components (sugars, proteins and fats), all sorts of salts are present: phosphates; salts of potassium, sodium, sulphur, magnesium, calcium, and chlorides and silicates; iron, copper, zinc, manganese, molybdenum, vanadium and other elements are present in very small, or trace quantities.

On the following page is shown the table compiled by Zellner and derived from Ceruti, which shows the relative amounts of substances in different dried toadstools. Remembering that each fresh toadstool is approximately nine-tenths water, it is necessary to divide each quoted figure by ten in order to obtain the relative amount in fresh material.

It is apparent from the table that toadstools are a relatively nutritious food. Fresh toadstools

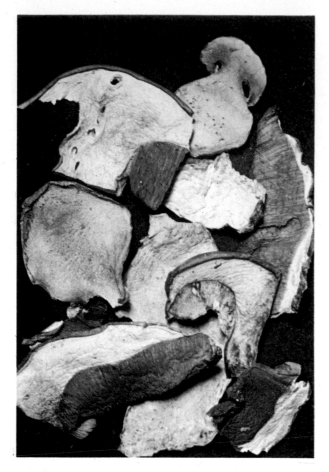

provide between 30 and 85 calories per 100 grams; dried toadstools yield between 300 and 360 calories per 100 grams. This figure is comparable with most vegetables, although it is only a tenth that of wheat-flour. Many vitamins are present in toadstools, especially niacin and vitamin D, but also present are the vitamins C, B^1, B^5, and B^6.

The following rules should be used when collecting toadstools for eating: first of all, they should be gathered in dry weather, after they have lost the dew and not immediately after rain. Young and small specimens should not be picked, since

In the photographs above, you can see how it is possible to identify fungi even when they are dried. Boletus edulis *(above left) can be distinguished from* Boletus luridus *(above) by its lighter colours*

they are often unidentifiable. Similarly, very old specimens should be avoided, as various processes of decomposition (which may produce poisonous substances) may have begun. Lastly, and perhaps obviously, mouldy or worm-eaten toadstools almost certainly should not be eaten and are best left alone.

Relative amounts of substances in dried toadstools					
Species	Proteins	Fats	Sugars	Myco-cellulose	Minerals
Boletus edulis (Cep)	40·00	2·00	34·00	6·78	7·47
Boletus scaber	37·43	4·70	17·09	31·45	8·17
Boletus luteus	36·65	5·11	20·64	28·52	8·96
Agaricus campestris (Field Mushroom)	43·47	1·72	40·05	9·63	5·50
Armillaria mellea (Honey Fungus)	27·50	4·92	18·42	37·58	10·92
Cantharallus cibarius (Chanterelle)	28·00	1·85	41·40	13·12	11·37
Hydnum repandum	24·45	4·64	47·40	14·00	9·42
Lycoperdon caelatum (puff-ball species)	55·98	2·99	19·18	14·42	7·90
Morchella esculenta (Common Morel)	34·12	2·37	46·83	6·89	8·97

Different toadstools may need to be gathered at different stages of development if they are to be preserved for future use. The ceps (boletes) should be collected when they are of medium size, while the Honey Fungus *(Armillaria mellea)* should be picked when young. They can be preserved in oil or vinegar. Other methods include pickling, which is particularly used in the food industry, and salting after boiling. A wide variety

Chanterelle, Cantharellus cibarius, *here enlarged to show the principal features, is an extremely tasty toadstool which is much sought after*

Many true agarics (Agaricus species) can safely be eaten when young and in perfect condition. This is the Horse Mushroom, Agaricus arvensis

of methods has been used for truffles, including immersing them in sand, bran, ashes, sawdust or maize-flour. They may even be put in fat, butter or wax, and brine and wine have also been used.

One of the commonest methods of preserving toadstools, however, is to dry them. The older methods involved placing the toadstools on trays or wires in the sun, ensuring that they are completely dried to prevent attack by insects and moulds. Generally, little taste is lost in this way, although truffles tend to lose some of their distinctive smell. More recently, mushrooms in particular have been dried by freeze-drying, which is rapid and very successful. This is now an important industrial process for the preservation of many foods. The dried mushrooms are then packed in sealed bags, keeping them dry and free from attack.

Poisoning by toadstools

This book shows only too clearly that there are many poisonous, and deadly, toadstools. These toadstools claim many victims each year. The species which cause the greatest number of fatalities or serious illnesses are generally those which are readily identified.

Even edible species may be poisonous if they start to decay, since substances called *ptomaines* may be produced, similar to those formed in decaying meat. The trouble may be caused not by the ptomaines themselves but by the bacteria associated with them. We are concerned with the symptoms caused by the poisons themselves.

The simplest type of poisoning is that involving the gut. This can be caused by any toadstool, no matter how innocuous, if enough of it is eaten or the person concerned suffers from gastric troubles. It is not surprising that eating a lot of one particular toadstool can cause trouble; they contain all sorts of unusual chemicals and the effect is rather like that on small boys who eat too many apples!

Large group of Lycoperdon perlatum (= L. gemmatum), *a* gasteromycete *common in fields and woods in autumn. The numerous spores released by these fruiting bodies can cause respiratory disease*

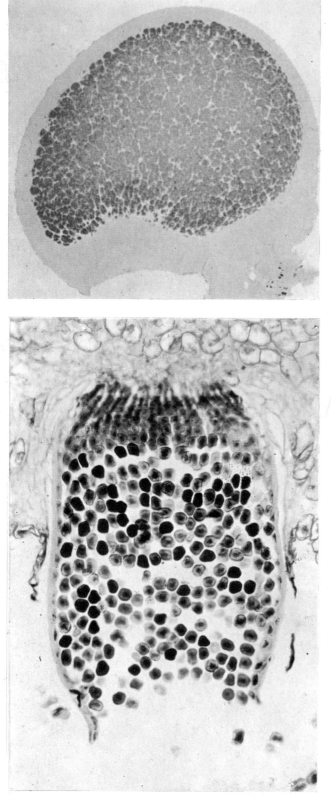

(Above left) stained section of a puff-ball (Lycoperdon *species) seen under a microscope. The brown, central mass (gleba) consists of numerous spores*

(Left) section of a reproductive cup of a rust (Puccinia *species) which causes disease in wheat and many other plants. The spores (which are red in this preparation) can cause respiratory troubles in man*

(Right) Amanita (=Amanitopsis) vaginata *var.* fulva *is edible if cooked*

Another factor which can account for individual poisoning is susceptibility or allergy to particular toadstools, which occurs just as it does when people cannot eat raspberries, or tuna or a host of other things. Unfortunately, there seems to be nothing that can be done about it. A certain amount is known about allergy to toadstools, but this knowledge is very limited because so few people eat toadstools other than the cultivated mushroom. The allergic reaction may take the form of intestinal pains or skin rashes.

Allergy to toadstools and other fungi may be caused not only by eating them, but also by breathing in the spores, on the same principle as in hay-fever caused by pollen grains. At certain times of the year the air is often loaded with fungal spores; they are always present in large numbers, but the level goes up and down seasonally. Both the small and large fungi produce enormous amounts of spores. The puff-balls (*Lycoperdon* species) release vast clouds of dark spores when ripe, and these spores can cause severe irritation

to the linings of the nose and throat.

Mention has been made in an earlier chapter of the effect of frost on toadstools, in particular on the Honey Fungus, which can become dangerous as a result of being frozen. Such toadstools should not be collected in late autumn, when the risk of frost is greatest. The same sort of effect results from very old specimens, particularly if the stalks are damaged at the base.

There are also certain toadstools and other fungi which should not be eaten raw; when cooked they may, however, be completely harmless. Among the *Ascomycetes* one may mention the morels (*Morchella* species), the false morels (*Helvella* species), various cup fungi *(Peziza)* and many others. Examples among the *Basidiomycetes* include *Amanita vaginata*; the Parasol Mushroom, *Lepiota procera* (especially old specimens); and *Armillaria (= Clitocybe) tabescens,* which may be confused with the closely related Honey Fungus. The coral fungi (*Clavaria* species) are sometimes poisonous even when cooked, and

the same can be said of *Paxillus involutus* and some of the boletes *(Boletus lividus* and *B. erythropus)*.

True poisoning, in the normal sense of the word, is a much more serious and different matter. In the less serious cases the symptoms are mainly gastroenteric, involving colic and vomiting; only rarely will death result from intestinal haemorrhage. The extent of the poisoning depends on a number of factors: on the individual sensitivity of the person; on the particular species; and on how much is eaten.

Among the toadstools which cause this type of poisoning are: *Rhodophyllus sinuatus* (distinguished from the mushrooms by the complete absence of a ring); the Devil's Boletus, *Boletus satanas*; the Yellow-staining Mushroom, *Agaricus xanthodermus; Hypholoma fasciculare* and

(Above left) Boletus miniatoporus *should not be eaten raw, and even after cooking should be consumed with caution*

(Right) Lepiota (= Macrolepiota) procera *is another species which should be eaten only when cooked; the stalks should be discarded*

H. sublateritium; and the Common Earth-ball, *Scleroderma aurantium*.

Many other species affect particularly susceptible people and these include the Clouded Clitocybe, *Clitocybe nebularis,* and *C. geotropa*; the Fairy Ring Champignon, *Marasmius oreades*; and the Spindle Shank, *Collybia fusipes*.

Toadstools with a bitter taste produce their own particular poisoning symptoms. Such toadstools

mainly belong to the russulas and lactarii, many of which are used in Eastern European countries as a substitute for pepper when dried and powdered. In the fresh fungus the chemicals responsible for the peppery taste are even more active, of course. If cooked for a long time, the toadstools lose their acrid taste.

A definite poisoning is caused by one of the false morel group, *Gyromitra esculenta* and also by related species of *Helvella*. These toadstools must not be eaten raw, although one may try a minute portion to test one's own susceptibility, since some people are not affected by them whereas others are. The active poison is helvellic acid, which is thermolabile (that is, it is destroyed by moderately high temperatures, in this case any above 60°C) and it is therefore destroyed by sufficient cooking. The action of this poison is to destroy red blood corpuscles.

(Above) Stropharia aeruginosa; *(below)* Stropharia ferii (= S. rugosoannulata); *both are of dubious edibility. They belong to a group of hallucinogens*

(Opposite, far left) an old clump of Honey Fungus, Armillaria mellea. *In this condition, it is essential to discard the stalks, which are very tough*

(Left and below left) Coprinus comatus *must not be consumed with alcohol*

Poisoning by *Gyromitra* and its relatives is only revealed 10–12 hours after eating, and involves sickness, sweating, diarrhoea and tremors. The poisonous qualities of these species are also destroyed by drying.

Similarly, a peculiar and distinctive form of poisoning can be shown by the Common Ink Cap, *Coprinus atramentarius*. It contains a substance which is particularly soluble in alcohol, so that any wine or other alcoholic drink which is drunk after a meal containing the Ink Cap brings on the symptoms: these include the face and other

(Above) Clavaria flava *may cause gastroenteric illness*

(Left) Russula emetica, *the Sickener, is aptly named and should be left well alone*

(Top right) the Fly Agaric, Amanita muscaria, *contains muscarine, a powerful poison*

(Below right) two Inocybe *species,* I. asterospora *(right) and* I. fastigiata *(far right), also contain muscarine-like poisons*

parts of the body becoming purple, together with increased heart-beat and gastric upsets. The effect can be shown some time after the meal, too, even as much as two days afterwards! This does not appear to happen with very young specimens.

Apart from the lethal effects of the Death Cap and its relatives, the most famous effect of toadstools on the human body is that caused by the various hallucinogenic toadstools: species of *Psilocybe* and *Stropharia* and probably also some of *Inocybe, Mycena* and *Paneolus*. The final effect of these fungi is, of course, delirium and hallucination, but it also involves reduced blood pressure (hypotension), sweating, and dilation of the pupils, accompanied by a feeling of intoxication and loss of weight.

Each species of hallucinogenic toadstool causes a variety of symptoms. The seriousness depends principally on the amount that has been eaten. In very serious cases delirium and state of anxiety may combine to drive the person to suicide.

The effects of these toadstools have been known for thousands of years, for example by the Mexican Indians, who employed them during religious and initiation ceremonies. In Mexico they are known as *teonanacatl*.

The most serious poisonings are caused by the Fly Agaric, and by the Death Cap and its relatives. The poison present in the Fly Agaric is known as muscarine and this chemical is also found in other, rarer toadstools such as *Amanita pantherina*, various *Inocybe* species (*I. fastigiata, I. patouillardi, I. umbrina* etc.), some *Clitocybe* species (*C. rivulosa, C. dealbata* etc.) and in *Russula emetica*. The poison is equally dangerous in all of them. *Amanita pantherina* is without doubt the most dangerous, having a definitely lethal effect since it contains a number of other poisons.

The effects of muscarine are shown quite quickly, and they include sweating, coupled with a cold feeling, heart murmurs, salivation, re-

(Above) Gyromitra esculenta *contains several poisons including helvellic acid*

(Below left) when young, the most poisonous toadstool, Amanita phalloides, *may easily be confused with edible species such as* A. vaginata *(below)*

(Below right) brown variety of Amanita phalloides *may also be confused with* A. citrina *(far right)*

striction of the pupils, vomiting, difficulty in breathing, drowsiness and hallucination. On its own it rarely causes death, though it may kill debilitated individuals or people who have eaten large amounts of the poison.

The poisons present in the Death Cap and its relatives are much more deadly and without special treatment are fairly certain to cause death even in small amounts. Of the three species concerned, the Death Cap is the most lethal, the other species are the Destroying Angel *(A. virosa)* and the Fool's Mushroom *(A. verna)*. Several poisons are involved. One of them, phalline (haemolysin) is destroyed by heat, but the others are not, so they will survive any amount of cooking. These include phalloidine and three amanitines, the latter being responsible for the principle effects on man and other animals. Unfortunately, the amanitines are not destroyed by the gastric juices. Only 0.1 mg of α-amanitine per kg of body weight is needed to cause death. Snails and slugs, however, are enormously resistant to amanitine, being able to tolerate up to 100 mg per kg of their weight, proportionately speaking of course! This is why anyone who has concluded that slug-eaten amanitas are safe to eat has suffered the consequences.

Poisoning by this *Amanita phalloides* group does not show up until some 10–30 (or even 48) hours after eating (rarely within 6–8 hours). The main effect is on the liver, which degenerates and causes the blood's sugar level to fall drastically,

Cortinarius
orellanus *is a highly
poisonous species*

together with side-effects on the kidneys and heart muscles.

The symptoms commence with violent, uncontrollable vomiting and gastric pains, diarrhoea and haemorrhage. This is followed by profuse sweating and dehydration, with consequent reduction of urine production, which eventually ceases altogether. The body becomes very cold, the face turns blue and the eyes appear sunken. The victim appears distraught with suffering, and the nervous system is generally affected.

As is common with various illnesses, the patient appears to be improving from time to time; the crises, however, become worse and worse. Although the heart beat is accelerated, it gradually becomes weaker until a state of coma is reached, during which the unfortunate victim dies.

Today, there are various treatments which seem to alleviate or cure the poisoning. These include injecting sugars and salts into the blood, and there is even a serum.

Some other toadstools can produce the same kind of symptoms. These species include *Cortinarius orellanus,* which up to about ten years ago was regarded as a harmless toadstool, as it is rather uncommon everywhere and is little known to most collectors. Nowadays, however, it is recognized as a truly deadly species. This change of opinion is due to the fact that the effects of the poisons are so slow to appear that it can take up to 160 days from the time of eating! With such an obvious need for careful examination of case histories, it is not surprising that this is a recent discovery.

Oddities among the toadstools

The toadstool world is so large and varied that it is not surprising to find a tremendous number of species which are curious in appearance or behaviour. Many of the curious species naturally belong to the moulds and other microscopic fungi, including the group which makes its living by capturing its food with small whips.

Our concern, however, is with the larger fungi among which there are many specimens which show interesting features. For example, how many

people are aware that some toadstools shine in the dark? This can be an eerie experience for anyone not aware of the phenomenon. Although such species are mainly found in woods, examples are known of toadstools which affect felled timber in timber yards. Occasionally, these toadstools have made people think that the stored wood is on fire. Among the woodland species which have this phosphorescence is the Honey Fungus, whose feeding strands make the tree glow. In some cases,

Larger fungi are parasitized by various smaller species. Here Asterophora parasitica (= Nyctalis asterophora) *is growing on an old russula*

for example *Pleurotus olearius* (=*Clitocybe olearia*), an associate of olive trees, the whole fungus glows.

This phosphorescence is caused by unstable, high-energy compounds which break down and produce light energy. A similar break-down produces very rapid colour changes.

It is odd to think of toadstools eating other toadstools, but this is shown in the case of *Boletus parasiticus,* which grows on the Common Earthball, *Scleroderma aurantium. Nyctalis (Asterophora) parasitica* attacks various *Russula* species, and can be found feeding from old specimens under the right conditions. There are species of *Cordyceps* which attack a wide variety of living organisms. *Cordyceps capitata* and *C. ophioglossoides* both attack false truffles, growing out of the ground in pine woods as drum-stick or club-shaped bodies up to 10 cm high. *Cordyceps militaris,* however, feeds off buried insect pupae.

The relationship between fungi and insects is, however, quite often beneficial to both sides. One unusual example is that of a *Stereum* species, the spores of which are stored by the female giant wood wasp *(Uroceras gigas)* in special glands. As the eggs are laid, spores of the *Stereum* are also injected into the wood. The spores germinate and digest the wood into a state more suited to the young wasp larvae.

These two pages show some of the smallest but most interesting Basidiomycetes of the Nidulariaceae: Crucibulum levis (above) and Cyathus olla (opposite, top and bottom). The cups contain a number of 'eggs' attached by a stalk. When it rains the 'eggs', containing numerous spores, are detached and splashed out

One of the most interesting groups of toadstools includes the Bird's Nest Fungi, *Crucibulum* and *Cyathus* species. They appear odd not only in their structure but also in the way in which they dispose of their spore masses. The fruiting body consists of a funnel-shaped cup, which is very small and contains a number of rounded structures. The whole thing does look remarkably like a minute nest with eggs. These species rely on rain for their spore dispersal; a rain drop landing in the cup detaches one or more of the 'eggs' (which are really masses of spores enclosed by a special skin) and splashes them out. Part of the 'egg' becomes attached to any suitable support, such as a blade of grass, and a specialized part of it entwines itself around the support. Even animals can act as suitable supports, carrying the spore masses for considerable distances. This odd mechanism may be spectacular, but it does not seem to be very successful since these toadstools are relatively uncommon.

The ways in which fungi feed	
Types of nutrition	**Food source**
Saprophytic	Feeding off dead materials. (Food much more difficult to digest, but no shortage)
Parasitic	Feeding off living organisms. (Some parasites continue as saprophytes when host is dead. Most are fairly specific, so there is often a shortage of hosts)
Symbiotic	Living closely with other organisms. (Both partners benefit. Most forest trees have a fungal mycorrhiza)

Selected Reading List

Alexopoulos, C. J. *Introductory Mycology*, John Wiley, New York and London, 1962, 1965.

Dennis, R. W. G. *British Cup Fungi and their Allies*, Ray Society, British Museum (Natural History), London, 1960.

Duddington, C. L. *Beginner's Guide to the Fungi*, Pelham Books, London, 1972; Drake Publications, New York, 1972.

Findlay, W. P. K. *Wayside and Woodland Fungi*, F. Warne, London and New York, 1967.

Kavaler, L. *Mushrooms, Moulds and Miracles*, John Day, New York, 1965; Harrap, London, 1967.

Lange, M. & Hora, F. B. *Guide to Mushrooms and Toadstools*, William Collins, Glasgow, 1963; Dutton, New York, 1963.

Large, E. C. *Advance of the Fungi*, Jonathan Cape, London, 1940; Dover, New York, 1940; Peter Smith, Gloucester, Mass. (reprint).

Ramsbottom, J. *Mushrooms and Toadstools* (New Naturalist Series), William Collins, Glasgow and New York, 1953, 1970.

Smith, A. H. *The Mushroom Hunter's Field Guide*, University of Michigan Press, Ann Arbor, 1963, 1971.

Wakefield, E. M. *The Observer's Book of Common Fungi*, F. Warne, London, 1954.

Acknowledgments

Acknowledgments of photographs from the following sources:
Archivio B: 91 bottom, 100 bottom, 109 bottom, 112; Archivio IGDA/Archivio B: 4, 29 bottom left and right, 65, 89 centre, 93, 100 top left, 110, 114 top and bottom; Archivio IGDA/P. Castano: 10; Bavestrelli, Bevilacqua, Prato: 66 top; Bevilacqua: 107 bottom; Bevilacqua, Prato: 27; S. C. Bisserot/Bruce Coleman: 84 top left, 87, 90, 105 bottom; R. B. Bock/Bruce Coleman: 86 bottom, 92 centre left, 105 top, 125; J. Burton/Bruce Coleman: 54 left; R. Longo: 91 centre, 92 top, 97, 108; A. Margiocco: 33; C. J. Ott/Bruce Coleman: 7 bottom, 32 top right, 82 bottom left; A. E. Mc. R. Pearce/Bruce Coleman: 126, 127 top; T. Poggio: 5, 11 top right, 21 top, 62 bottom, 71, 82 top; S. C. Porter/Bruce Coleman: 2, 6 top, 8, 9 top, 11 top left and bottom, 19 bottom, 21 bottom, 37 top, 38 bottom right, 39 top, 42 bottom left, 53 top, 80 bottom, 82 bottom right, 83, 86 top right, 91 top, 92 centre left, 95 bottom, 96 top, 102, 118 bottom, 119 top, 123 right, 127 bottom; S.E.F.: 38 bottom left; J. Six: 6 bottom, 7 top, 14 right, 17 bottom, 23, 29 top, 32 top left, 34, 40 bottom, 42 bottom right, 45 bottom, 59 centre, 63 top left, 68, 70 bottom left and right, 75 top, 78, 81 bottom left and right, 84 bottom, 88, 89 top and centre, 92 right, 99, 104, 107 top, 111, 115, 116, 121 top, 122 bottom left, 123 bottom left; Tomsich: 113; S. Viola: 9 bottom, 13, 14 left, 15, 16, 18, 19 top, 20, 24, 25, 26, 28, 32 bottom left and right, 35, 36, 37 bottom left, 39 bottom, 40 top, 41, 42 top, 43, 44, 45 top, 46, 47, 49 bottom left and right, 50, 51 left, 52, 53 bottom left and right, 55, 56, 57, 58, 59 top, 60, 61, 62 top, 63 top right, bottom left and right, 66 bottom, 67, 69, 70 top, 73, 74 top left, 77, 79, 80 top, 81 top left, 86 top left, 89 bottom, 94, 95 top, 96 bottom, 98, 101, 117, 119 bottom, 120 bottom, 121 bottom left and right, 122 bottom right, 124; W. H. D. Wince/Bruce Coleman: 1, 54 right, 82 centre left, 118 top right.
Drawings by Luciana Biagini.